My
OneNote® 2016

Sherry Kinkoph Gunter

que®

800 East 96th Street,
Indianapolis, Indiana 46240 USA

My OneNote® 2016

Copyright © 2016 by Pearson Education

ISBN-13: 978-0-7897-5520-9
ISBN-10: 0-7897-5520-3

Library of Congress Control Number: 2015949957

Printed in the United States of America

First Printing: November 2015

Trademarks

All terms mentioned in this book that are known to be trademarks or service marks have been appropriately capitalized. Que Publishing cannot attest to the accuracy of this information. Use of a term in this book should not be regarded as affecting the validity of any trademark or service mark.

Warning and Disclaimer

Every effort has been made to make this book as complete and as accurate as possible, but no warranty or fitness is implied. The information provided is on an "as is" basis. The author and the publisher shall have neither liability nor responsibility to any person or entity with respect to any loss or damages arising from the information contained in this book or from the use of the programs accompanying it.

Special Sales

For information about buying this title in bulk quantities, or for special sales opportunities (which may include electronic versions; custom cover designs; and content particular to your business, training goals, marketing focus, or branding interests), please contact our corporate sales department at corpsales@pearsoned.com or (800) 382-3419.

For government sales inquiries, please contact governmentsales@pearsoned.com.

For questions about sales outside the U.S., please contact international@pearsoned.com.

Editor-in-Chief
Greg Wiegand

Acquisitions Editor
Michelle Newcomb

Development Editor
Ginny Munroe

Managing Editor
Kristy Hart

Senior Project Editor
Betsy Gratner

Copy Editor
Geneil Breeze

Indexer
Erika Millen

Proofreader
Kathy Ruiz

Technical Editor
Faithe Wempen

Editorial Assistant
Cindy Teeters

Cover Designer
Mark Shirar

Compositor
Nonie Ratcliff

Contributor
Michael Miller

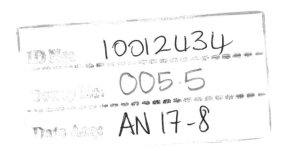

Contents at a Glance

Table of Contents

3   **Working with Sections, Pages, and Subpages**   **51**

About the Author

Sherry Kinkoph Gunter has written and edited oodles of books over the past 23 years covering a wide variety of computer topics, including Microsoft Office programs, social media, digital photography, and web applications. Her recent titles include *Sams Teach Yourself Facebook*, *Absolute Beginner's Guide to Word 2013*, and *My Google Apps*. Sherry began writing computer books back in 1992, and her flexible writing style has allowed her to author for a varied assortment of imprints and formats. Sherry's ongoing quest is to aid users of all levels in the mastering of ever-changing computer technologies, helping users make sense of it all and get the most out of their machines and online experiences. Sherry currently resides in a swamp in the wilds of east central Indiana with a lovable ogre and a menagerie of interesting creatures.

Dedication

To my favorite shopping sisters, Candi Noland and Kathy Privett—may you always find the best bargains.

Acknowledgments

Special thanks go out to Michelle Newcomb for thinking of me for this project; to development editor Ginny Munroe, for her dedication and patience in shepherding this book; to copy editor Geneil Breeze, for ensuring that all the i's were dotted and t's were crossed; to technical editor Faithe Wempen and project editor Betsy Gratner, for offering valuable input along the way; last-minute thanks to Mike Miller, for assisting with several of the chapters without a moment's notice; and finally a big round of applause for the entire production team and their able talents in creating and assembling this book.

We Want to Hear from You!

As the reader of this book, *you* are our most important critic and commentator. We value your opinion and want to know what we're doing right, what we could do better, what areas you'd like to see us publish in, and any other words of wisdom you're willing to pass our way.

We welcome your comments. You can email or write to let us know what you did or didn't like about this book—as well as what we can do to make our books better.

Please note that we cannot help you with technical problems related to the topic of this book.

When you write, please be sure to include this book's title and author as well as your name and email address. We will carefully review your comments and share them with the author and editors who worked on the book.

Email: feedback@quepublishing.com

Mail: Que Publishing
ATTN: Reader Feedback
800 East 96th Street
Indianapolis, IN 46240 USA

Reader Services

Register your copy of *My OneNote 2016* at informit.com for convenient access to downloads, updates, and corrections as they become available. To start the registration process, go to informit.com/register and log in or create an account.* Enter the product ISBN, 9780789755209, and click submit. Once the process is complete, you will find any available bonus content under "Registered Products."

*Be sure to check the box that you would like to hear from us in order to receive exclusive discounts on future editions of this product.

Notebook name   **Section tabs**   **Pages**

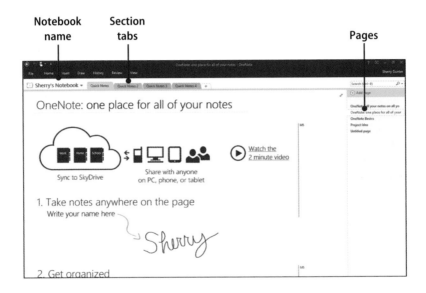

In this prologue, you're introduced to Microsoft OneNote 2016, the note-taking app that takes notes and organization to a whole new level. Topics include

→ Learning how OneNote works

→ Finding out what you can do with OneNote

→ Previewing features and tools

→ Learning about differences in the OneNote app and the full-featured program

What Is OneNote?

Microsoft OneNote is a personal information management application—PIM for short—designed to help you gather notes of all kinds into one convenient digital notebook. By *notes*, we're talking about anything you want to jot down or keep track of in a digital environment, such as web page clippings, lists, photos, classroom lectures, video clips, work meeting scribbles, brainstorming ideas, and so much more. You can easily organize your notes any way you want, and best of all, share them with others or sync them across devices so they're always at your fingertips.

OneNote is a powerful tool, but it's often overlooked in the Microsoft Office suite of programs. If you've never used the program before, you're about to find out how useful it can be. If you're already a OneNote user, you'll quickly get up to speed on using the newest version, OneNote 2016. Since it's available for free, what better time than now to learn how to put it to work for you?

Introducing OneNote

Microsoft OneNote has been around since 2003. Microsoft started bundling OneNote with the Office suite of programs and today it's part of the new Office 2016. As of 2015, OneNote is also available as a free stand-alone app for Windows, Mac, Windows Phone, iOS, and Android. If you use OneDrive or Office Online, it's available as a web-based application too. Basically, you can use OneNote across a variety of platforms and devices, with or without the Microsoft Office suite.

Like a lot of software, OneNote's name pretty much describes its purpose—taking notes. Whether you're making notes for work, taking notes in a class, or simply gathering information for a home project, OneNote can help. Notes can be any kind of information you typically write down, draw out, or find on the Internet. Rather than use sticky notes and paper notebooks to create notes, you can use OneNote as a digital organizer and take notes on your computer, tablet, or smartphone. For example, let's say you're in charge of a large work project involving many different parts that require you to keep track of appointments, meeting notes, ideas, resources, conversations, email correspondence, to-do lists, and more. All this information is bound to make a cluttered desk at work. OneNote helps you organize it all in one safe spot—electronically speaking. Plus, with cloud storage, you can access the information from anywhere as long as you have an Internet connection.

OneNote organizes data into digital notebooks, just like a binder, complete with pages and sections for additional organizing. In fact, the program window looks rather like a real notebook, with color-coded section tabs to flip between pages of notes. You can add as many notes as you want to a page, including text notes you type in, notes you draw directly onto a touch-screen surface, links to web pages, items you copy and paste, and video or audio you record. You can even use OneNote 2016 to take pictures of your computer screen and save them as notes. Much like an actual notebook page, you can place your notes wherever you want on the page, without any layout or structure restrictions. OneNote automatically saves everything you add to a notebook so you don't have to worry about looking for a Save button or trying to remember to save a file before closing the program window.

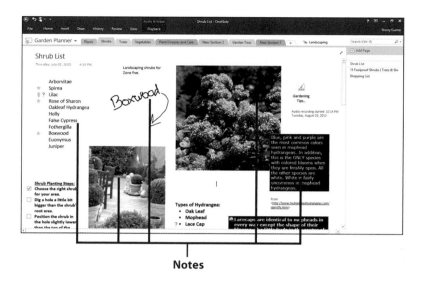

Notes

How Do I Find OneNote?

OneNote is available with the Microsoft Office suite, or you can download it for free as a stand-alone app. If you haven't installed OneNote yet, you can find it on the Microsoft website: www.onenote.com. If you're not sure whether you have OneNote 2016 installed or an older version or app version, you can conduct a search for OneNote 2016 on your computer. For example, if you're using Windows 10, you can use Cortana (the Windows 10 digital personal assistant and knowledge navigator) to search for installed versions of OneNote.

What Can I Do with OneNote?

Obviously, taking notes is OneNote's main function, but notes aren't just things you write down. Notes can be many types of data and used for all kinds of purposes. When it comes right down to it, OneNote can help you organize almost any aspect of your work or home life. Need some examples? Here are a few real life scenarios of things you can do with OneNote:

- Use OneNote to plan and organize your next big family vacation. Collect links to potential destinations, pictures of fun spots to visit, travel ideas from friends and family members, booking contact information, flight information, and final itinerary lists. Keep tabs on the budget and record expenses as you go.

- Keep track of school projects, due dates, and tests. Use OneNote with Microsoft Outlook to coordinate calendar dates. Link a OneNote notebook to your PowerPoint presentation file so you can update content or convert a OneNote notebook into a Word file format to share with a teacher or fellow project collaborator.

- Prepare work projects, compiling notes, phone calls, ideas, and deadlines. Keep related emails in one spot for easy revisiting. You can also store your notebook file in a place where other users can access it, like on a shared network or cloud location. You can control access with password-protection for specific data or assign a password to the entire file.

- Stay on top of a home remodeling project by creating a Home Restoration notebook. Create sections for subjects like Ideas, Budget, Contractors, Calendar Timeline, and organize information into pages like Roofing, Flooring, Cabinets, and Paint. You might collect video clips for remodeling tasks you can do yourself and store them in a section labeled DIY.

- Be your own wedding planner with OneNote. Collect links to your favorite wedding sites, organize pictures of wedding attire and hair styles, check your budget using an embedded spreadsheet, scribble down ideas about the ceremony, and make lists of local cake decorators, florists, and photographers. Use subpages to compile photo posing ideas and locations, floral arrangement pictures, and cake ideas.

Are you beginning to see the potential OneNote offers? Unlike a paper notebook that quickly becomes packed with pages, scrap papers, and pictures, your digital notebook expands to fit all the information you want to document. You can use OneNote online and offline to help you manage whatever type of projects you are working on. Whether you're sitting at home with your laptop or desktop computer, or on the go with your smartphone or tablet, you can tap into OneNote's power and organize your world, whatever that entails.

Apps That Work with OneNote

You can find additional apps that work with OneNote, such as CloudHQ, which helps you synchronize your notebooks with other popular cloud services (like Dropbox and Evernote). For a full list of additional apps and devices, visit the OneNote website at www.onenote.com.

Exploring OneNote Features

OneNote offers a variety of tools and features you can use to create and work with notes, many ways to share and access your notes, and numerous methods for interacting with your notebooks. Here are just a few to consider:

- Dock the OneNote window to the side of your desktop so it's easy to view and work with notes while performing other tasks.

- Install a browser add-in, called OneNote Clipper, that offers quick tools for clipping web content and placing it in a notebook.

- Use the Screen Clipping tool to clip whatever you're viewing onscreen and send it to a notebook.

- Sync your notebooks across multiple devices. Store your notebooks on Microsoft OneDrive or another cloud service and access them from any computer, laptop, tablet, or smartphone.

- Share your notebooks directly with others, such as a project team or coworkers, or put them on a SharePoint site or OneDrive so everyone can access them and work on them at the same time.

- Embed all kinds of items into your notebook pages, including audio and video clips, photos, and files.

- Record audio notes instead of text notes during a class or meeting. You can also add notes during important parts of the recording session and revisit them quickly later via links to the recording.

OneNote tools are found on the Ribbon

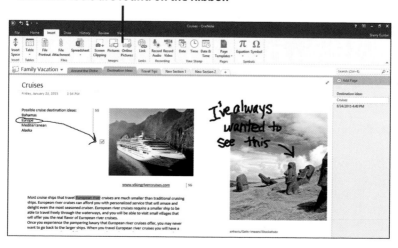

- Tag important items in your notes for easy searching and sorting later. You can even create a summary page of tags for easy reference.

- Tap into OneNote's search capabilities to search your notes, including searching for text in photos, audio, and video files.

- Apply a template. OneNote offers all kinds of templates you can assign to your notebook pages. You can find templates for students, work projects, or decorative designs to suit your fancy.

- Turn your handwriting into note text using OneNote's OCR (optical character recognition) technology and a touchscreen computer or device.

- Jot down math equations with a stylus or your finger on a touchscreen, and the Ink Equation converter turns the scribbles into typed mathematical equations.

- Integrate OneNote with other Microsoft Office programs. OneNote works seamlessly with Office 2016, particularly with Outlook. You can flag a note and turn it into an Outlook task, or email notebook pages to others complete with all the formatting intact.

OneNote File Formats

OneNote 2010, 2013, and 2016 all use the same file format (.ONE), so if you have notebooks from the 2010 or 2013 program versions, you can easily open and edit them in OneNote 2016. Unfortunately, newer notebooks are not backward-compatible, so you cannot use a notebook you create in OneNote 2016 in the OneNote 2007 program, for example. You can, however, convert older notebook files into the newer notebook file format.

Comparing OneNotes

Not all versions of OneNote are the same. There are several "flavors" of OneNote available: the desktop program (OneNote 2016), an app version, and a web-based version. Let's take a minute and go over which one is which.

The OneNote 2016 desktop program is the newest version of OneNote. OneNote 2016 is what this book is all about, but you might have another version of OneNote on your computer or device, called the OneNote app. The OneNote app is installed with Windows 8, 8.1, and 10. It's a little different than the desktop version of the program. The desktop version is clearly labeled OneNote 2016, whereas the app version just says OneNote.

For example, if you're using Windows 8 or 8.1, you can find a OneNote tile on the Start screen. Windows 10 users will find the same tile listed on the Start menu. The OneNote tile, when activated, opens a slightly different version of the program, configured much like the app for a smartphone or tablet. In fact, it's actually called the OneNote app. The app version is optimized for use on tablets and mobile devices.

You can use the OneNote app to view and work with notebooks; some of the features and tools from OneNote 2016 may not be available, however. The app version of the program displays onscreen items in a different layout, with pages and sections listed on the left side of the window and no ribbon of tools to access.

The app version of OneNote

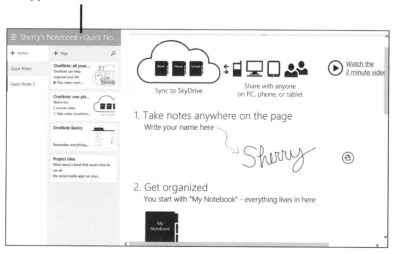

There's also a web version of OneNote. The Microsoft Office programs, including OneNote, are available as web-based applications—programs that run in a web browser. Called OneNote Online, the web-based version is easy to access from any device, and any notebooks you are storing in the cloud can be viewed and edited from the browser window. OneNote Online also differs slightly from OneNote 2016, but the basics are still the same.

The web version of OneNote

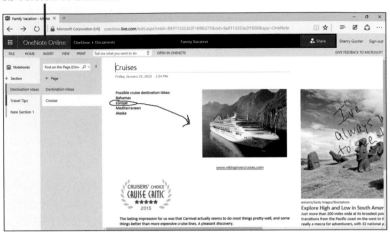

All these variations of OneNote might seem a little confusing at first, but they offer you a variety of ways to access and work with your notebooks. You might find yourself using OneNote 2016 to build your notebooks on your PC, for example, and the OneNote app on your smartphone when you're out and about. Here's a scenario you might consider: Let's say you're using a OneNote notebook to collect notes and information for a building project for your house. Such a notebook is probably filled with ideas, pictures, do-it-yourself articles, and links. You might use your laptop, for instance, to create a list of items you need to buy at the store in your project notebook. If you store the notebook on Microsoft's OneDrive (cloud storage), you can access the same notebook using the OneNote app handy on your smartphone with a Wi-Fi connection. This keeps the project shopping list, along with all the other project notes, at your fingertips when you go to the store.

So how do you tell the difference between the app and the full-blown program when trying to open OneNote? You can distinguish between the OneNote app and the OneNote program based on the icon and label you see listed in the Start menu. The icons look slightly different, and the desktop version is distinctly labeled OneNote 2016.

**OneNote
app icon**

**OneNote
program icon**

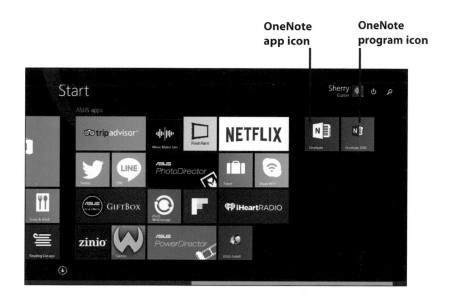

The content of this book focuses primarily on the desktop version of OneNote 2016. You can still use many of the tasks in the app version and the web-based version, but the desktop program version offers so much more in terms of tools and features.

Now that you know what OneNote does and have a few ideas for putting it to use, it's time to start learning how the program works. For the rest of the book, the screenshots you see illustrate how the program works on the Windows platform; if you use OneNote on other platforms, your screens will differ. You may also experience differences in some of the features and tools, but the basics are always the same. If you're using a touchscreen device, you can utilize touch gestures to activate OneNote commands and features, such as tapping the screen to activate a tool or swiping left or right to pan your view. Ready to get started? Let's go!

Screen view modes

Ribbon

Program window controls

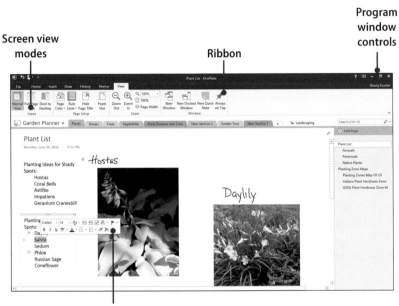

Mini toolbar

In this chapter, you learn about the Microsoft OneNote program window and how to start using the program's various features. Topics include

→ Opening and closing the application

→ Navigating around the OneNote workspace

→ Discovering how to find commands on the Ribbon, toolbars, and shortcut menus

→ Changing screen view and magnification

→ Finding help with OneNote issues and features

Getting Started with OneNote

Before you jump in and start trying to immediately create and gather notes, it's a good idea to take a moment or two and familiarize yourself with the program window and its basics. Basics include tasks you can use to enhance your experience using the program, such as learning how to zoom in or out to change your view, or how to find all the important commands you need to work with notes. Learning your way around the OneNote program window up front can save you time and effort later.

Opening and Closing OneNote

OneNote 2016 opens and closes just like any other program on your computer. In most cases, you simply activate the OneNote icon to start things rolling. For example, depending on various installations and computer systems, OneNote 2016 may have installed with the Microsoft Office suite, or you may have added OneNote as a stand-alone program. If so, the OneNote 2016 icon you are looking for may appear in the Start menu in Windows 10 (click All apps to locate the program alphabetically), among the tiles on Windows 8.1, or among the programs listed on the Start menu's All Programs menu group in Windows 7.

Once the program is open, you can leave it running in the background while working with other programs, and then add notes whenever you need to.

>>>Go Further

COMPARING ONENOTES

As you learned in the Prologue, not all versions of OneNote you encounter are the same, and you need to discern which OneNote icon represents the version you want to use when opening OneNote from the Start screen, Start menu, or desktop. For example, Windows 8.1 and 10 users have access to the OneNote app, an optimized version of OneNote designed specifically for tablet and smartphone use, but also for use with computers and laptops. The OneNote app appears as a tile among the default apps (Windows 8 and 8.1) and on the Start menu (Windows 10). When opened, the app features a different layout than the full version of OneNote (OneNote 2016), and it doesn't offer a ribbon of commands and tools.

Don't worry, you can still view and work with all your notebooks in both versions. Just keep in mind that some of the features and tools may not be available in the app. The content of this book focuses on the desktop version of OneNote (OneNote 2016).

Open OneNote in Windows 8.1

The procedure you use to open OneNote depends on what operating platform or device you're using. The first time you use OneNote 2016, the default notebook opens showing tips and examples about how to use the program. Use these steps if you're a Windows 8.1 user.

1. Click or tap the Windows Start button.

2. Click or tap All Apps.

3. Scroll through the apps list and click or tap OneNote 2016.

4. The program opens in its own window. Click or tap a video to play an instructional tip.

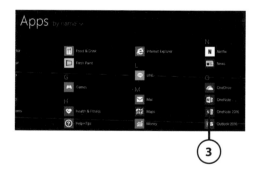

Signing In

Depending on your setup, you may be prompted to sign in to your Microsoft account before opening OneNote. This typically involves entering your email address, password, and a verification code (sent either by email or text message). Just follow the onscreen prompts as directed.

Windows 7

If you're using Windows 7, you can open OneNote through the Windows Start menu. Click the Start button, click All Programs, and then scroll to the OneNote 2016 program icon and select it.

Open OneNote in Windows 10

In Windows 10, programs are listed in the All apps menu list. You can scroll through the list to find the OneNote 2016 program. The first time you use OneNote, the default notebook opens with tips and examples on how to use the program.

1. Click or tap the Start menu.

2. Click or tap All apps.

3. Scroll through the apps list and click or tap OneNote 2016.

Which OneNote?

OneNote is available in two "flavors"—the OneNote 2016 program and the OneNote app. The icons used to represent each vary slightly in appearance. OneNote 2016 is the full-featured program you can install on your computer, laptop, or tablet, or use the web version (as part of the Microsoft Office suite). The OneNote app is an optimized version for tablet and smartphone users (computer users can use the app as well). The app version looks different, and not all the features are available; however, you can perform many of the same tasks explained in this book. The content of this book focuses on OneNote 2016.

4. The program opens in its own window. Click or tap a video link to view an instructional video clip about using the program.

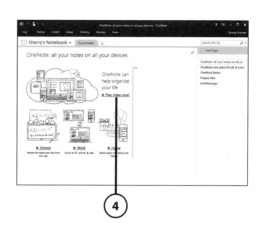

④

Pin It

Do you want speedier access to OneNote? You can pin the OneNote 2016 program to the Start menu in Windows 8, 8.1, or 10. Just right-click or press and hold the OneNote 2016 program name that appears in the All apps list and click or tap Pin to Start.

Close OneNote

You can close OneNote when you're completely finished with your note-taking tasks. You don't have to worry about saving your work. OneNote automatically saves your notes and any open notebooks you're currently using.

1. Click or tap the Close button to close the program window.

①

Other Closing Methods

You can also right-click or press and hold anywhere on the OneNote 2016 title bar area to display a shortcut menu and choose Close. You can also press Alt+4 on the keyboard to close the program.

Navigating the OneNote Workspace

OneNote is designed to look a lot like an actual notebook but displayed in a digital format. The program window features a lean, clean workspace without a lot of clutter. This leaves you plenty of room for adding and working with notes. OneNote employs an interface similar to the other Microsoft Office programs, with Ribbon tabs of tools accessible from the top of the window, program window controls (always located in the top-right corner), and a Quick Access Toolbar.

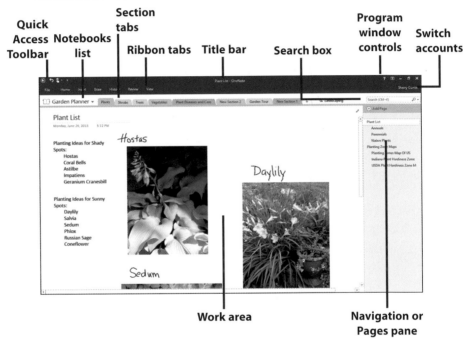

Let's take a look at all the elements viewable in the program window and how they work:

Title bar   Displays the program name and the current notebook open.

Quick Access Toolbar   Use this toolbar to quickly perform common tasks, such as undoing an action or printing. Click or tap the arrow icon at the end of the bar to view more commands you can display.

Ribbon   Click or tap a Ribbon tab to view associated tools and commands.

Search box   Use this feature to find anything in your notebooks.

Program window controls   Use these icon buttons to control the window display, such as minimizing, maximizing, or closing the window.

Switch accounts   Click or tap your account ID to switch between accounts or change the account settings.

Notebooks list   Use this drop-down list to view your open notebooks.

Section tabs   Click or tap a tab to view a section in your notebook.

Navigation or Pages pane   Use this pane to navigate pages, add new pages, and view subpages.

Work area   The middle of the program window is where you do all your actual note taking, whether typing text, writing onscreen, or inserting pictures or files.

You learn more about using these various elements in the pages to come.

Extra Quick Access Toolbar Icon

If you're using a touchscreen, you see an extra icon displayed on the Quick Access Toolbar for switching between mouse display mode or touch display mode. The icon is called the Optimize Spacing between Commands button (its icon looks like a finger pointing at a button), and you can click or tap the icon to toggle the command to add or remove extra spacing around tools for easier tapping or clicking onscreen.

Use the Default Notebook

OneNote starts you out with a default notebook labeled with your name and offering all kinds of tips on how to use the program, including several embedded instructional videos you can watch. It's worth your while to glance through the available information and try out some of the techniques where instructed.

1. If the default notebook is not already open, click or tap File.

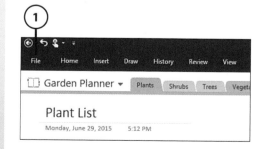

2. Locate the notebook with your user name on it; click or tap View Notebook.

3. The notebook opens with several pages of instructions and demos. Click or tap a Play button to play a video clip.

4. Click or tap a page to view another topic.

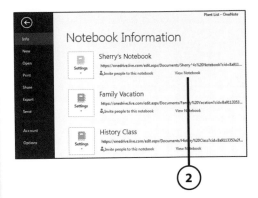

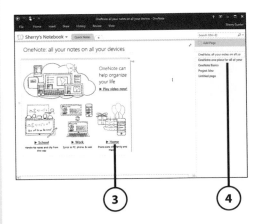

Minimize or Maximize the Window

You can use the Minimize and Maximize buttons to minimize the program window or make it fill the screen. Minimizing gets the window out of the way so you can view other apps you're using or the desktop. Maximizing resizes the window to its maximum size again.

1. To minimize the program window, click or tap the Minimize button.

2. To display the window again, click or tap the OneNote icon on the taskbar.

3. To resize the window smaller, click or tap the Restore Down button.

4. To maximize the window, click or
tap the Maximize button.

Docking OneNote
You can also dock the OneNote
program window so it remains
open and in view while you work
with other programs and apps.
You learn more about docking the
window later in this chapter.

Working with the Ribbon

OneNote's Ribbon organizes commands and features into tabs listed across
the top of the program window. The Ribbon format is common throughout
the Microsoft Office programs. When you display a tab, it appears much like
a ribbon of tools across the top of the program window. Related command
buttons and features are organized into groups found within each tab. Some
commands are buttons; others are drop-down menus or lists of options you
can select, called *galleries*. If you see an arrow icon next to a command, it lists
additional options you can choose from when activated. Some commands
also open additional dialog boxes with more options to choose from.

Drop-down menu   **Gallery**

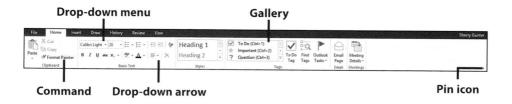

Command   **Drop-down arrow**   **Pin icon**

The File tab is the only tab that opens a completely different screen rather
than just a ribbon of commands; use the File tab when you want to create
new notebooks, open existing notebooks, print, email, locate account
options, and other file-related tasks.

By default, the Ribbon is collapsed to just the tab names, freeing up more room to work on your notes. You can pin the Ribbon in place, if you want, to keep the commands displayed. The Pin icon lets you pin the Ribbon open and you can easily unpin it again to close it.

Use the Ribbon

Using the Ribbon is intuitive and straightforward. Since commands are grouped logically according to type, you can expect to find, for example, drawing tools on the Draw tab and viewing features on the View tab.

1. Click or tap the tab you want to view.

2. The Ribbon opens; click or tap the command or feature you want to use.

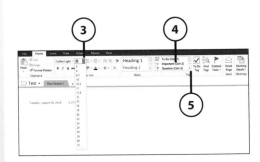

3. To display a drop-down menu, click or tap the arrow and make a selection from the menu.

4. To make a selection from a gallery box, click or tap the selection.

5. To view more gallery items, click or tap the More button.

6. The gallery expands as a list; click or tap to make a selection.

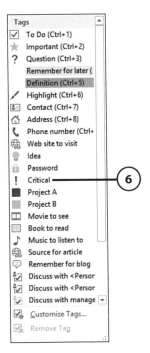

Different Buttons on the Home Tab!

If you are also using Outlook 2016 (another program in the Microsoft Office suite), your OneNote 2016 Home tab features two additional buttons for setting up Outlook tasks and meetings. If you're not using Outlook, these two buttons are not present.

Pin the Ribbon

To keep the Ribbon displayed at all times, you can pin it in place. You can always collapse it again when you need to.

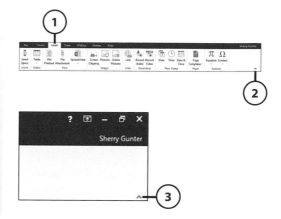

1. Click or tap any tab.

2. Click or tap the Pin the Ribbon icon.

3. To unpin the Ribbon again, click or tap the Collapse the Ribbon icon.

>>>Go Further

CUSTOMIZING THE RIBBON

You can add or subtract commands among the Ribbon's tabs to suit the way you work. To find the customizing options, right-click or press and hold an empty area on the Ribbon and click or tap Customize the Ribbon from the shortcut menu that appears. This opens the OneNote Options dialog box to the Customize Ribbon controls where you can find lists of commands to add or subtract, options for creating new Ribbon tabs, and a reset option if you want to return all the customizing options back to the default settings. You can learn more about customizing the Ribbon in Chapter 13, "Customizing OneNote."

Working with Toolbars and Shortcut Menus

In addition to commands you find on the Ribbon, you can also activate commands via toolbars. Toolbars display command buttons you can click or tap to activate a tool or feature. The Quick Access Toolbar sits in the upper-left corner of the program window offering a small group of icon buttons for common commands. By default, the Quick Access Toolbar displays the Back and Undo commands. You can turn on other commands in the display as needed using the menu's drop-down arrow.

Quick Access Toolbar buttons toggle on or off ———

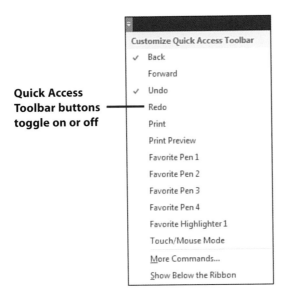

Other toolbars may pop up from time to time when you select text or other items on your notebook pages. These context toolbars list commands related to the task you're working on at the time. For example, if you select note text, a pop-up toolbar, called the Mini toolbar, of formatting tools appears. You can easily bold text or change the font using the command buttons. If you ignore the toolbar and keep working, it disappears after a few seconds.

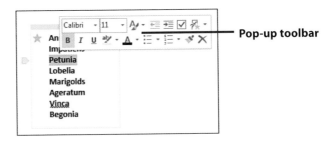

Pop-up toolbar

Right-clicking (or pressing and holding if you're a touchscreen user) areas of the OneNote screen may bring up a shortcut menu, also called a *context menu*. This type of menu offers a list of commands related to what you're doing. For example, if you right-click a picture, the menu offers tools for rotating and resizing the picture, among other options.

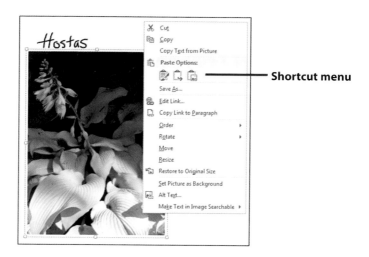

Shortcut menu

Use the Quick Access Toolbar

The Quick Access Toolbar starts out with several default commands displayed on the toolbar. You can add more to the display, as needed or turn off commands you don't need.

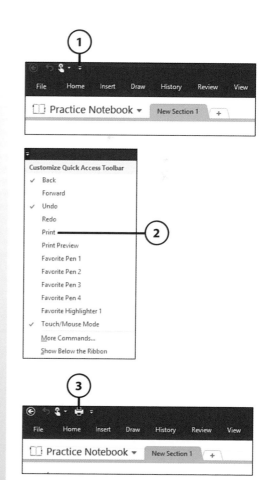

1. Click or tap the Customize Quick Access Toolbar drop-down arrow.

2. Click or tap the command you want to view on the toolbar (a check mark indicates which commands already appear on the toolbar).

3. OneNote adds the command to the display. In this example, the Print command is added. To activate the new command, click or tap it.

Use Mini Toolbars

Pop-up toolbars, also called Mini toolbars, typically spring into action when you select text or other items in a notebook. When a Mini toolbar appears, you can utilize the available commands. If you don't need them, you can continue working and the toolbar fades from view.

1. With the Mini toolbar in view, click or tap the command you want to apply.

2. OneNote immediately applies the command to the selected item or items (in this example, bullets are added to the selected note text). The Mini toolbar remains open for additional selections; click or tap an additional tool, if needed.

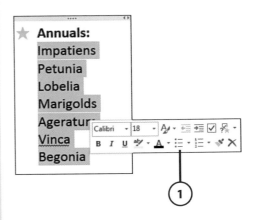

Outlook Tasks

If you have Outlook 2016 installed, your Mini toolbar includes a button for marking note text as an Outlook task. If you're not using Outlook, the Outlook Tasks button is not present.

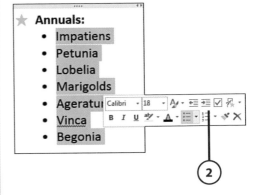

Right-Click It

You can also right-click or press and hold to display a Mini toolbar related to the task at hand. For example, if you right-click over note text, a context menu appears with commands along with the Mini toolbar.

Use Context Menus

You can use context or shortcut menus to access commands related to the task at hand.

1. Right-click or press and hold to display a shortcut menu.

2. Click or tap the command you want to apply.

3. OneNote immediately applies the command and closes the shortcut menu.

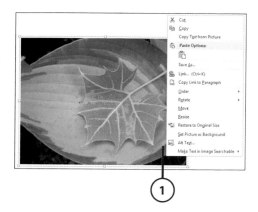

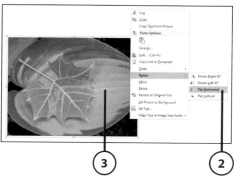

Changing Screen Views

You can change the way you look at your notes and notebooks onscreen. You can also adjust the zoom level, or magnification, of your notebook workspace to view more or less of your notebook on the screen. View modes and document zooming are handy features when you want to get a different view of your notes, such as zooming in to make the note text easier to read onscreen or switching to Full Page view to free up more workspace for adding notes. You can find all of OneNote's viewing tools on the Ribbon's View tab.

Zoom In or Out

Magnifying tools have long been a staple of most programs, allowing users to zoom in for a closer look or zoom out for a bird's eye view of a page. A quick click or tap of the Zoom Out and Zoom In buttons let you quickly change page magnification. You can also specify an exact magnification setting for the zoom.

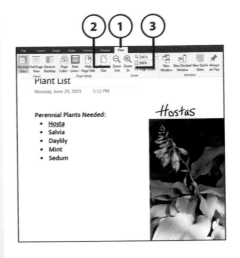

1. Click or tap the Ribbon's View tab.

2. To zoom out, click or tap Zoom Out.

3. To zoom in, click or tap Zoom In.

4. To view the notebook at 100%, click or tap the 100% command.

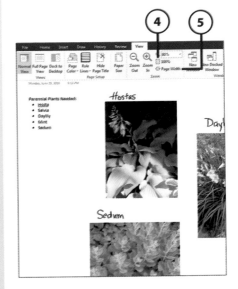

5. To match the page width to the window width, click or tap Page Width.

6. To specify an exact magnification or choose from a list of options, click or tap the Zoom drop-down arrow.

7. Click or tap a percentage.

Type It In

You can also type an exact magnification percentage directly into the Zoom text box. Simply click or tap the box and enter a value.

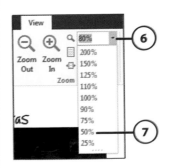

Switch View Modes

OneNote offers three view modes: Normal (the default view), Full Page, and Dock to Desktop (which you learn about next). You can switch to Full Page view when you don't want to see anything in the program window but your notes. OneNote hides the Ribbon bar, title bar, program window controls, and Pages pane, leaving you plenty of room to work.

1. Click or tap the Ribbon's View tab.

2. Click or tap Full Page View.

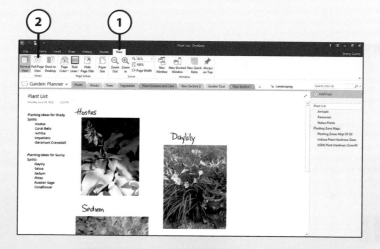

3. OneNote hides the window elements and displays more of your notebook.

4. To return to Normal view again, click or tap Normal View.

Toggle It

You can also toggle back and forth between Normal and Full Page views without the View tab. While in Normal view, click or tap the Full Page View icon located in the upper-right corner of the page (just to the left of the Pages pane).

Dock OneNote to the Desktop

You can dock the OneNote program window so it sits beside all the other program and app windows you open, ready to use at a moment's notice. Docking OneNote is helpful when you're taking notes from a browser window. You can easily glance back and forth between the two open windows, copy and paste notes and links, and more.

1. Click or tap the Ribbon's View tab.

2. Click or tap Dock to Desktop.

3. OneNote docks itself on the right side of the screen. You can open other programs or apps as desired and view them while still using OneNote.

4. To access the Ribbon commands, click or tap the three dots at the top of the screen.

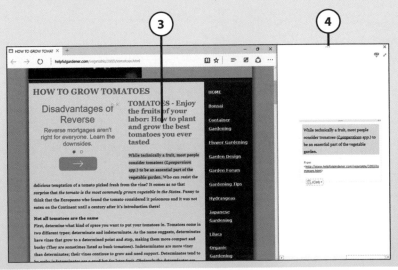

5. To return to Normal view mode, click or tap the View tab.

6. Click or tap Normal View.

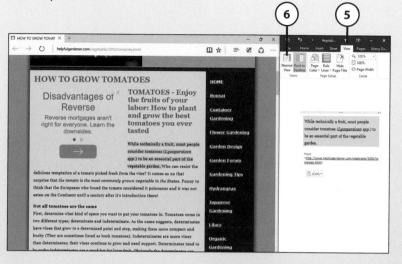

Shortcut

You can also click or tap the Normal View icon located in the upper-right corner of the docked program window to return to the Normal View mode.

Finding Help with OneNote Issues and Topics

If you ever need extra help with the OneNote program, you can seek help through the OneNote Help feature. When activated, Help opens a special window you can use to look up topics, search online for additional resources, and generally learn more about the program or feature you are working with at the time. With an online connection, Help taps into resources from the Microsoft Office website. Help offers tutorials, links to related topics, and a table of contents you can peruse.

Open Help

You can use OneNote's Help resources to look up topics to help you use the program and its features. The following steps show you how to open Help:

1. Click or tap the Help icon.

2. The OneNote Help window opens; click or tap the Search box and type in a topic or issue.

3. Press Enter or click or tap the Search icon.

4. The Help window displays any matching results; click or tap a topic.

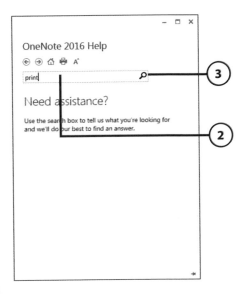

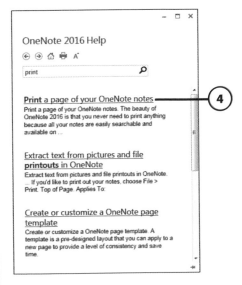

5. Information about the topic appears; you can resize the window or click or tap Maximize for easier reading.

6. With some topics you view, additional links are available to learn about related topics; click or tap a link to view another information page.

7. Use the Back and Forward navigation buttons to move back and forth between pages you view.

8. To return to the main Help window again, click or tap Home.

9. To exit Help, click or tap the Close button.

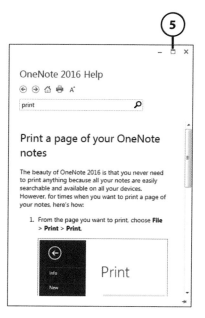

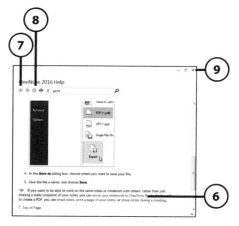

Use Backstage View to work with open notebooks.

Open notebooks are listed here.

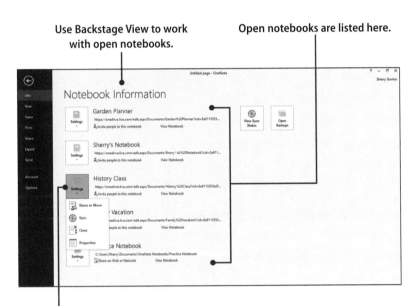

Use the Settings button to view notebook settings.

In this chapter, you discover how notebooks work in OneNote, including how to start new notebooks as well as remove old notebooks you no longer use. Topics include

→ Learning how notebooks are structured
→ Creating new notebooks
→ Opening and closing existing notebooks
→ Removing old notebooks

2

Working with Notebooks

Notebooks are the holders of all your note-taking efforts in Microsoft OneNote. Much like a folder holds files or a document holds text, a notebook holds all the items you deem worthy as notes. In fact, you can think of a notebook as a specialized folder of sorts, but with its own interface and unique tools. A notebook automatically expands and saves all the content you place into it, without any effort on your part. All you have to do is decide how you want to organize your notes and where to place them on a page. You can create as many notebooks as you want, and you never have to worry about running out of paper. It's so easy, you might find yourself keeping notebooks for all kinds of projects you hadn't previously thought about. Because you can quickly sync them across devices, your notebooks can always go where you go. You can print them out, email them, or share them with others; there's really no end to their usage, whether for home, work, or school.

Exploring Notebooks

Items you collect and store digitally with OneNote are placed into notebooks. Much like a regular spiral paper notebook, your digital notebooks are built page by page, and you can organize pages into sections. When you create a notebook, OneNote starts you out with a single, blank page. You can start adding notes anywhere on the page and add as many sections and pages as you want.

Take a look at the notebook structure as it appears onscreen:

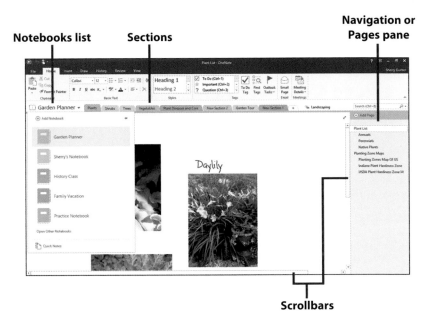

Here's a rundown of the notebook elements:

Notebooks list The current notebook name appears here, and you can quickly switch between other open notebooks using the drop-down menu.

Sections Across the top of the notebook are tabs for each section you add. To jump to a section, just click or tap the section tab. You can give the tabs unique names, too, so you can easily figure out what each contains.

Navigation or Pages pane On the right side of the program window is a pane listing pages you add, along with a command for adding new pages. You can use this pane to navigate between pages in a notebook.

Scrollbars   The more content you add to a page, the longer or wider the page becomes. You can use the scrollbars to move up and down or left and right.

The behind-the-scenes action for working with notebooks happens when you click or tap the File tab on the Ribbon. A whole screen of notebook information opens, along with commands for printing, sharing, exporting, and emailing notebooks. You can use this screen, also called *Backstage View*, to view your notebooks, sync them to your cloud storage, view file properties, and close any open notebooks you're finished using. The Info tab appears by default and displays Notebook Information. Click or tap the other tabs to view their contents.

The Info tab lists notebooks you're using.

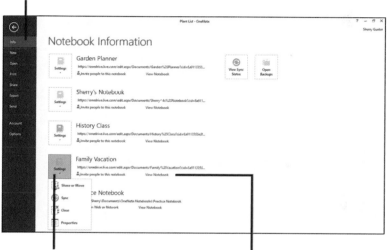

Use the Settings button to   **Click here to view a**
access more commands.   **notebook.**

Backstage View is also where you go to create new notebooks or open existing notebooks from other locations.

Know Your File Type

OneNote notebooks are stored with the .ONE file extension. This format supports notebook files from OneNote 2010-2013. If you have existing notebooks created in earlier versions of OneNote, you can convert them to the newest format (2010–2016). Learn more about this process later in the chapter.

Creating New Notebooks

When you create new files in most programs, such as Microsoft Word or Excel, a new blank file opens ready for you to add data. Later, when you save the file, you choose a filename and a storage destination, such as a folder or drive on your computer or a location on your cloud service. OneNote does things a little differently. You choose a storage location and a filename at the same time you create the new notebook. Because you don't have to worry about saving the notebook file (saving is automatic), OneNote skips the file saving and naming step that normally happens after you start a new file and lets you determine a location for the notebook at the same time you create the file.

As previously mentioned, you can create as many notebooks as you want in OneNote. When creating a new notebook, the New Notebook window is displayed. You use this window to assign a name for the notebook file.

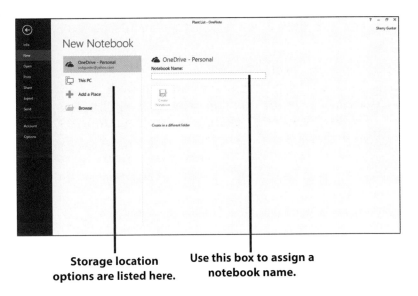

Storage location options are listed here.   **Use this box to assign a notebook name.**

The left side of the window lists location options. You can use several of the options listed to navigate to a particular drive or folder on your computer or you can opt to utilize cloud storage in which to store the notebook. Storage options include the following:

OneDrive   Store your notebook in OneDrive's top-level folder when you select this option. If you prefer to put the notebook in another folder on OneDrive, choose the Create in a Different Folder link.

This PC   Use this option to store the notebook in the default OneNote Notebooks folder in your computer's Documents Library. If you prefer a different location, choose the Create in a Different Folder link.

Add a Place   Hopefully, you're already using Microsoft's OneDrive cloud storage. If not, you can add it using this option and store your notebook there. If you're using SharePoint, you can use this option to store the notebook on Office 365 SharePoint.

Browse   Use this option to store the notebook in a recent folder or browse for a particular folder or drive.

Depending on which option you pick, additional dialog boxes or settings may appear for you to narrow down a location. For example, you can click or tap the Browse option and navigate to the exact folder or drive where you want to save the notebook.

If you store your notebooks on your computer or laptop, they're automatically saved in a default folder in your Documents folder unless you specify another location. Look for a OneNote Notebooks folder to find your notebooks.

If you want your notebooks easily accessible from any device, your best bet is to store your notebooks on OneDrive (or Office 365 SharePoint). Your OneDrive files are private unless you choose to share them with other users. If an Internet connection isn't always possible, you can always sync them to the cloud at a later time.

>>>Go Further
WHAT IS ONEDRIVE?

OneDrive is Microsoft's online cloud storage service. It's automatically part of your Microsoft account, and if you're not already using it to store your files online, it's ready and waiting for you. You can access it using your Microsoft account ID and password. OneDrive includes 15GB data you can store, whether it's documents, spreadsheets, pictures—any type of file you want kept in the cloud can be stored on OneDrive. The real beauty of online storage is you can access the files from any device. Wherever and whenever you're using an Internet connection, you can view and work with your OneDrive files, upload and download, move them around, and more.

You can navigate to your OneDrive account using a web browser (visit OneDrive.live.com). You can also access the files through Microsoft Office programs such as OneNote. OneNote automatically syncs with your cloud account, and you can quickly and easily work with any notebooks you store online. To learn more about using OneDrive, see Chapter 14, "Taking OneNote Online."

Create a New Notebook

You can create a new notebook and specify where to store it, such as on OneDrive or in a particular folder on your computer.

1. On the Ribbon, click or tap the File tab.

2. Click or tap New.

3. Choose a location for the notebook.

4. Type a notebook name in the Notebook Name box.

5. Click or tap Create Notebook.

6. If you're storing the notebook on OneDrive, a prompt box appears asking whether you want to share the notebook with others; click or tap Not Now to continue without sharing.

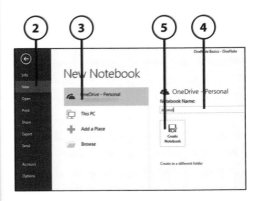

7. OneNote opens your new note-book. You can now start entering notes.

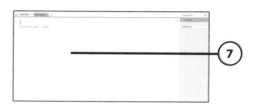

Sharing Notebooks Already?

You can learn more about shar-ing notebooks in Chapter 12, "Distributing and Sharing Notes." If you do want to go ahead and share the notebook, OneNote switches you over to the Share tab in Backstage View, and you can enter the email addresses of people you're sharing with.

Assign a Notebook Color

You can assign a color to a note-book name making it easier to identify notebooks listed among the Notebooks list or the Notebook Information window. For example, you might color coordinate all your work-related notebooks as one color and all your personal notebooks as another color.

1. Click or tap the Notebooks list.

2. Right-click or press and hold the notebook name.

3. Click or tap Properties.

4. Click or tap the Color drop-down arrow.

5. Click or tap a color.

6. Click or tap OK.

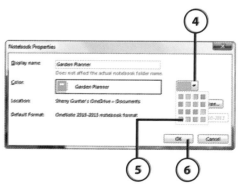

7. OneNote changes the notebook color; to view the new color, click or tap the Notebooks list.

Opening and Closing Notebooks

You can open and close notebooks as needed. Notebooks stay open until you close them. As you add and work with more notebooks, they tend to clutter the list or sidebar, especially if you're using the OneNote app on a smartphone or tablet. Closing notebooks might also help if you need to switch between two or three notebooks without having to deal with all the other open notebooks. On the other hand, you might prefer to have two or three important notebooks open at all times.

Close Notebooks

You can use the Notebook Information window in Backstage View to close notebooks. The window lists all the open notebooks and options for working with each one, including closing them. When you close a notebook, it's no longer shown in the Notebooks list in the program window.

1. Click or tap File.

2. From the Info tab, click or tap the Settings button for the first notebook you want to close.

3. Click or tap Close. OneNote closes the notebook file.

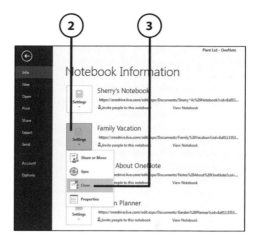

Close Notebooks with the Shortcut Menu

You can quickly close a notebook using the shortcut menu without having to display the Notebook Information window in Backstage View. The context menu offers commands related specifically to notebooks, such as syncing and sharing.

1. Click or tap the Notebooks list.

2. Right-click (or press and hold if you're using your finger or stylus on a touchscreen) over the notebook you want to close.

3. Click or tap Close this Notebook.

Use Normal View

To use the shortcut menu to close notebooks, make sure you're viewing notebooks in Normal view mode. See Chapter 1, "Getting Started with OneNote," to learn more about view modes in OneNote.

Open a Notebook

You can open a notebook using the Open Notebook window. Depending on the notebook's location, you may need to navigate to the particular notebook you want to use.

1. Click or tap File.

2. Click or tap Open.

3. To open a notebook from OneDrive, click or tap the notebook name from this list.

4. OneNote keeps a list of recently used notebooks handy here; click or tap a notebook from the list.

5. To open a notebook from another location, click or tap the location and navigate to the file.

Manage OneDrive Notebooks

Are you using your Microsoft account's free cloud storage to store your notebooks? You can click or tap the Manage Notebooks on OneDrive link listed below the OneDrive notebook list to open your browser window to your OneDrive account. You can view and work with files stored in the cloud using this link. Learn more about cloud storage and keeping notebooks on the Internet in Chapter 14.

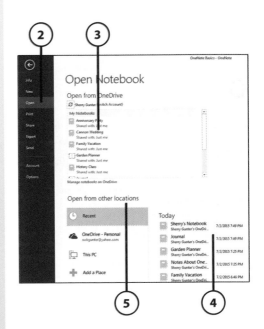

>>>*Go Further*

CONVERTING NOTEBOOKS

If you have older notebooks from previous versions of OneNote, you can convert them to the latest format. For example, if you have a notebook created with OneNote 2003, you can upgrade it and use it in OneNote 2016. OneNote 2010, 2013, and 2016 all use the same file format, so if you have notebooks from 2010 or 2013, they should be good to go in OneNote 2016. Unfortunately, newer notebooks are not backward-compatible, so you cannot use a notebook you create in OneNote 2016 in the OneNote 2007 program, for example. To convert a notebook, click or tap File to open Backstage view. From the Info tab, click the Settings button for the notebook and choose Properties. Then click Convert to 2010-2016.

Deleting Notebooks

Deleting notebooks isn't as easy as you might think. You won't find a Delete command to use in OneNote. Instead, you must use File Explorer (or Windows Explorer for Windows 7 users) to remove a notebook. Mac users can use Finder to remove the notebook. If the notebook is in the cloud, you can log on to your OneDrive account to delete the file. When you delete a notebook, it's moved to the Recycle Bin where you can permanently remove it. Any items in the notebook aren't recoverable once you delete the notebook from the Recycle Bin.

Delete a Notebook from Your Computer

You can delete a notebook you keep stored on your computer using Windows File Explorer. When you delete a locally stored notebook in File Explorer, it's removed to the Windows Recycle Bin, where all deleted files and folders go. The notebook is not permanently gone until you empty the Recycle Bin.

1. Open File Explorer (or Windows Explorer if you're a Windows 7 user); click or tap the File Explorer icon on the taskbar.

2. Navigate to the notebook file you want to remove.

3. Right-click or press and hold the notebook name.

4. Click or tap Delete from the shortcut menu.

5. To permanently remove the file, right-click or press and hold the Recycle Bin icon.

6. Click or tap Empty Recycle Bin.

7. A warning prompt box appears; click or tap Yes to delete the file(s).

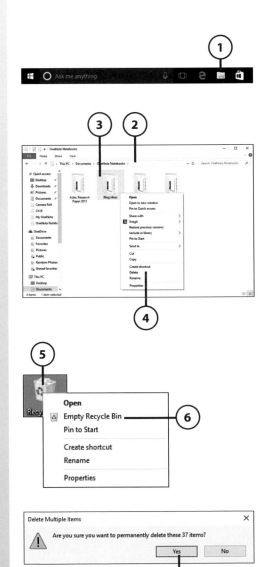

Delete a Notebook from OneDrive

You can remove notebooks you no longer need from your cloud storage using OneDrive's Delete button. Files and folders you delete on OneDrive are moved to the online Recycle Bin. Keep in mind that anyone you shared the notebook with can no longer access the file either.

1. Open OneDrive.

2. Navigate to the notebook file you want to remove.

3. Move the mouse pointer over the notebook name and click or tap the check box.

4. Click or tap Delete and the file is immediately removed.

5. To permanently remove the notebook from your cloud storage, click or tap the Menu button.

6. Click or tap Recycle bin.

More About OneDrive

To learn more about using OneDrive to store your notebooks, see Chapter 14.

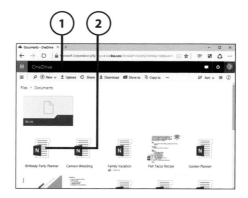

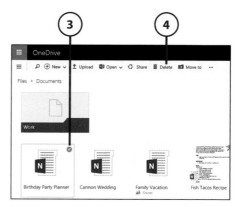

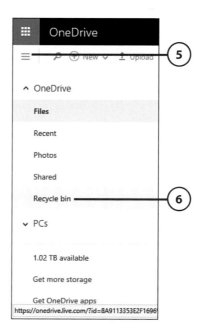

7. Click or tap the notebook check box.

8. Click or tap Delete.

9. A warning prompt box appears; click or tap Delete to delete the notebook.

Where's the Delete?

If your window size is narrow, you may not see the Delete button when you select the notebook file you want to remove. Click or tap the More button (three dots) to expand the commands and view the Delete command.

OneDrive Shortcut

If you want to navigate to OneDrive from within the OneNote 2016 program window to manage your online notebooks, you can use Backstage view. Click or tap File, then click or tap the Open tab. Next, click or tap the Manage Notebooks on OneDrive link listed below the OneDrive notebook list. This opens your browser window to your OneDrive account where you can view your online content.

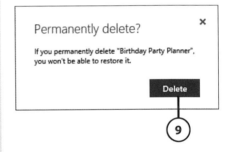

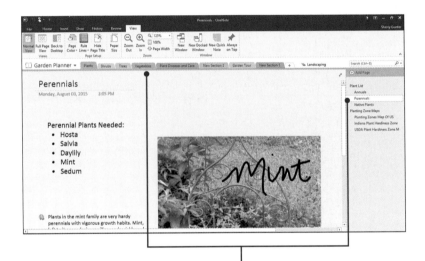

Notebook structure is built with sections and pages.

This chapter covers all the basics for building your notebook structure. Topics include

→ Adding and naming sections
→ Grouping sections
→ Assigning passwords to sensitive section information
→ Adding pages to your notebook
→ Moving and copying pages
→ Creating subpages
→ Assigning templates to pages

Working with Sections, Pages, and Subpages

Paper notebooks, such as three-ring binders, typically utilize a few common things: paper pages, dividers to create sections, and pockets to fill with loose sheets of paper, like handouts or index cards. Users can rearrange the pages and sections as needed. After awhile, though, pages fall out, paper holes rip and fray, and notes are lost among the many pages bulging out of the notebook. Paper notebooks are also easily lost or misplaced.

Digital notebooks employ a similar organizational setup—pages and sections—but you never have to worry about losing a piece of paper or running out of room, and you can also conduct an easy search to find what you're looking for among your notes. In fact, the only thing really missing from a OneNote notebook is a digital notebook cover so you can write your name on it. Who needs a notebook cover, though, when your notebooks are always with you as long as you have an Internet connection? In this chapter, you learn the basics of how to construct your notebooks to suit the way you like to take and keep notes.

Storing Notes with Sections, Pages, and Subpages

Digital notebooks in OneNote are organized into *sections* and *pages*. Just like a paper notebook might have section tabs, your OneNote notebook uses section tabs to help divide information where needed. Each section can contain numerous pages. In fact, the entire notebook can expand as much as you require.

As you're viewing your notebook, sections are displayed as tabs across the top of the notebook. Every new notebook you create starts out with one section and a blank page in that section. Sections let you focus on particular topics or interests. You can add more sections as you build your notebook. For example, if you're creating a notebook focused on retirement planning, you might include sections like Budget, Goals, Income Streams, and so on. To view and work with a particular section, just click or tap its tab. You can assign names to the notebook tabs to help identify what each section contains. You can also color-code section tabs to help you more easily identify or separate the contents.

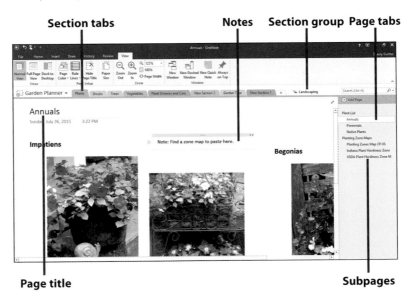

In each section, you can add pages. OneNote starts you out with a blank page for every section you create. Pages appear listed on the right side of the program window in their own special navigation area (unless you're using OneNote Online, in which case they're on the left side). The page tab area lists all the pages found in the current section in a column layout. Page tabs listed work just like section tabs; click or tap a page tab to view its contents.

You can give a page a title at the top, if you want, and OneNote automatically inserts a date below the title area so you know when the page was first created. You can edit the date, too.

You can place as many notes on a page as you want; there's no limit and you can't run out of space. You can use scrollbars to move around a page to view, add, and edit notes.

You can make pages subordinate to other pages, thus creating *subpages*. For example, if you're building a notebook of vacation ideas, you might have a main section for Destinations and create pages for topics like Cruises and Resorts. Then, among these pages, you might have subpages for types of cruises and resorts, such as European Cruises, Mediterranean Cruises, Caribbean Cruises, and so on.

As you're working with sections and pages, you might find yourself needing to delete content you no longer want included in a notebook, such as an extra page you added or a section that's no longer relevant to the notebook's purpose. The Delete command comes in handy for instantly removing content. However, what if you find out later that you accidentally deleted something important? OneNote has a feature to help you recover pages and sections you removed. OneNote places deleted sections and pages in a special holding area called the Notebook Recycle Bin. It keeps them there for up to 60 days, hopefully plenty of time to retrieve a page or section when you need it. After 60 days, the sections and pages are removed permanently. Tucked away on the Ribbon's History tab, the Notebook Recycle Bin works rather like the Windows Recycle Bin on your desktop but holds deleted sections and pages instead of files and folders. Each notebook you create has its own Notebook Recycle Bin. When you display the bin's contents, you can move or copy a deleted page or section to restore it to the current notebook or a completely different notebook. The Notebook Recycle Bin does not keep discarded notes, such as text notes or pictures but only works with pages and sections you remove.

OneNote Remembers

As you work with various notebooks in OneNote, the program remembers which sections and pages you were viewing during your last session. The next time you open the file, you can pick up where you left off.

Working with Sections

Sections make great organizing tools in OneNote. You can use sections to keep related notes and pages together. You can add as many sections as you want to a notebook, as well as move their order around, rename or color the tabs, and remove sections you no longer need. You can even merge sections and group them in a notebook.

Add a Section

Adding a section is as easy as a click or tap. The Create a New Section button is always on hand for quickly inserting new sections into your notebooks.

1. Click or tap Create a New Section.

2. OneNote adds an empty section to the notebook. You can name the section or use the default name; type a new name, if needed.

New Section Shortcuts
You can also add a section by right-clicking or pressing and holding a tab and choosing New Section from the shortcut menu that appears. Another shortcut is to press Ctrl+T on the keyboard.

Rename a Section

Give your sections unique names to help you identify their contents. For example, since sections can contain numerous pages, you might want to assign a name that encompasses the types of pages a section holds.

1. Double-click or double-tap the section tab.

2. Type in a name for the section and press Enter/Return.

3. The new name is assigned.

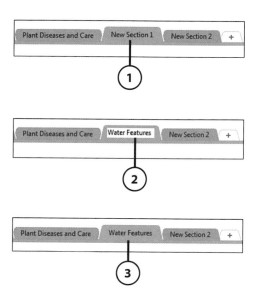

Assign a Tab Color

By default, OneNote varies the color between sections you add. You can choose your own color schemes. For example, you might make all the summary sections for a research paper yellow. The color you assign to a section also colors the page tab area on the right side of the notebook window.

1. Right-click or press and hold a section tab.

2. Click or tap Section Color.

3. Click or tap a color from the menu list.

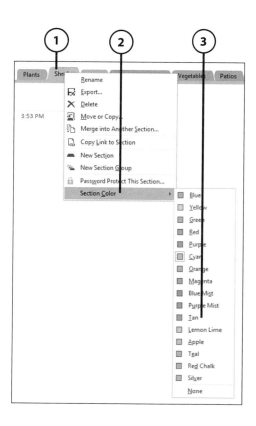

4. OneNote assigns the new color to the tab.

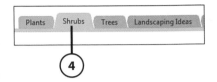

No Color

If you prefer no color for your section tabs, click or tap the None option in the menu list. OneNote displays the default program window color for the tab instead.

Move a Section

You can reorder your notebook sections to suit your own organizational structure.

1. Drag a section tab and drop it where you want it to appear. An arrow icon marks the insertion spot as you drag.

2. OneNote moves the section.

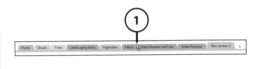

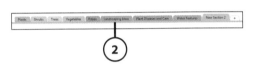

Moving Sections to Other Sections

You can use the Move or Copy command to move a section to another notebook. Right-click or press and hold the section tab and choose Move or Copy from the shortcut menu. Next, click or tap the notebook to which you want to move the section and click or tap Move.

Delete a Section

You can remove a section you no longer need in your notebook. Doing so removes any notes and pages the section includes, so make sure you truly want to remove the section before applying the Delete command. Any sections you delete are moved to the notebook's Notebook Recycle Bin where they remain recoverable for up to 60 days.

1. Right-click or press and hold a section tab.

2. Click or tap Delete.

3. A prompt box appears; click or tap Yes to complete the removal process.

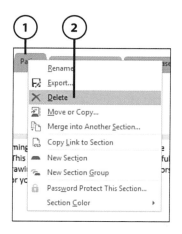

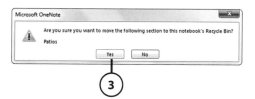

>>>Go Further

RESTORING A DELETED SECTION

The Notebook Recycle Bin is a temporary holding spot for deleted sections and pages. You can recover deleted sections from your notebook's Notebook Recycle Bin for as long as 60 days after you first deleted them, but only if you haven't already manually removed them by emptying the Notebook Recycle Bin.

To recover a section, you must first open the Notebook Recycle Bin. Oddly enough, the bin presents discarded sections and pages in a notebook layout, just like a regular notebook. The only difference is noted in the notebook's name—the bin uses the current notebook's name and adds "OneNote Recycle Bin" to the label. Deleted sections are listed across the top of the Notebook Recycle Bin and deleted pages are listed in the Pages pane.

To display the Notebook Recycle Bin, click or tap the History tab and then click or tap the Notebook Recycle Bin drop-down arrow. Next, click or tap Notebook Recycle Bin to open the bin as a notebook of deleted sections and pages. To recover a page or section, right-click the section or page tab and use the Move or Copy command to move the item back to the current notebook or choose another notebook location. When you activate the Move or Copy command, the Move or Copy Pages dialog box opens and you can select a specific notebook or section to restore to and then move or copy the section or page.

Empty the Notebook Recycle Bin

Notebook sections you delete are moved to the Notebook Recycle Bin. Each notebook has its own Recycle Bin, making it easy to retrieve sections you accidentally removed. OneNote keeps deleted pages and sections for 60 days. They're automatically deleted after that, or you can manually delete them as outlined in these steps. Only manually delete sections if you're sure you don't need them again. Manually emptying the bin can free up computer space.

1. Click or tap the History tab.

2. Click or tap the Notebook Recycle Bin arrow.

3. Click or tap Empty Recycle Bin.

4. A prompt box appears; click or tap Yes to empty the Recycle Bin.

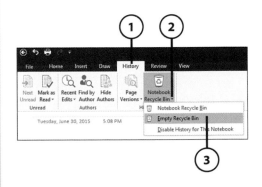

Grouping Sections

If you find your notebook window filling up with too many sections to view at a glance, you can group the sections to keep related information together. Think of section groups as an extra layer of organization you can add to a notebook.

1. Right-click or press and hold any section tab.

2. Click or tap New Section Group.

3. The new group appears to the right of the section tabs; type a name for the group and press Enter/Return.

4. To view a group's contents, click or tap the group name.

5. The new group opens; click or tap Create a New Section to add new sections to the group.

6. Click or tap the Navigate to Parent Section Group to return to the main section group.

Plant Diseases and Care | Water Features | New Section 2 | +

- Rename
- Export...
- X Delete
- Move or Copy...
- Merge into Another Section...
- Copy Link to Section
- New Section
- New Section Group
- Password Protect This Section...
- Section Color ▶

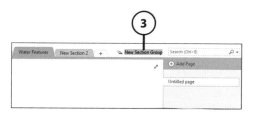

Water Features | New Section 2 | + | New Section Group | Search (Ctrl+E)
Add Page
Untitled page

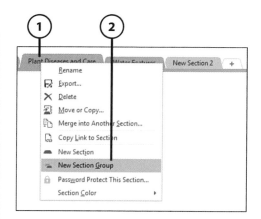

New Section 2 | + | Landscaping

Garden Planner
Landscaping ▼ 5 | +

There aren't any sections here.

Click here to add a section.

Move a Section to a Group

You can move a section to a group or out of a group using the Move or Copy command.

1. Right-click or press and hold the section tab.

2. Click or tap Move or Copy.

3. Click or tap the section you want to move the section to.

4. Click or tap Move.

5. OneNote moves the section and all of its content to the designated group.

6. Click or tap Navigate to Parent Section Group to return to the main sections.

Copying a Section

The occasion may arise when you need to copy a section instead of just move it. The Move or Copy command comes into play again, but instead of clicking or tapping the Move button in the Move or Copy Section dialog box, click or tap Copy.

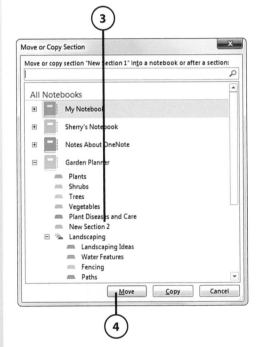

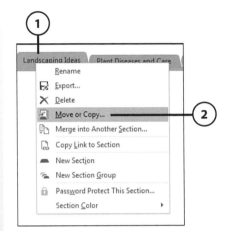

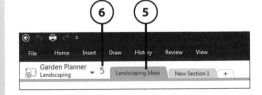

Merge a Section

You can combine a section with an existing section using the Merge Section feature.

1. Right-click or press and hold the section tab for the section you want to merge.

2. Click or tap Merge into Another Section.

3. Click or tap the section you want to merge with.

4. Click or tap Merge.

5. A prompt box appears; click or tap Merge Sections to continue.

6. Another prompt box appears; click or tap to choose whether to delete the original section.

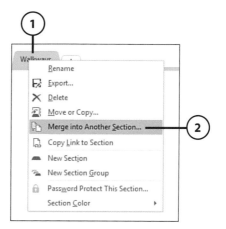

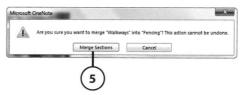

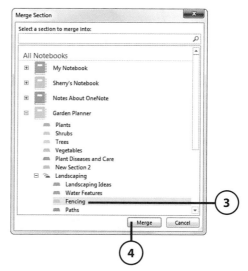

7. OneNote merges the section and adds the content as a page in the designated section.

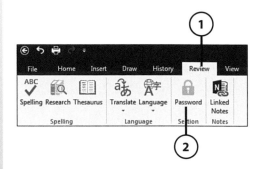

Assign a Password to a Section

If a section in your notebook contains sensitive information, you can assign a password for that section. This protects all the pages found within that section. Be sure to keep your new password in a safe place. If you lose it or forget it, you will not be able to access the notebook section again.

1. Display the section you want to assign a password to and click or tap Review.

2. Click or tap Password.

3. Click or tap Set Password.

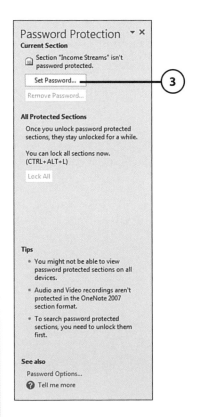

4. Type in a password.

5. Retype the password.

6. Click or tap OK.

7. If there are backup copies of the file, a prompt box appears; OneNote warns you that any existing backup copies of the notebook are not password protected. You can choose to delete those now if you want or keep them as is; click or tap your selection.

8. Click or tap the Close icon to close the Password Protection pane.

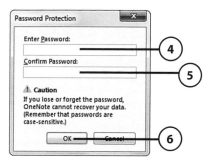

Removing Passwords

Revisit the Password Protection pane when you want to remove or change a password. Use the Remove Password button to undo any password associated with the section, or use the Change Password button to reset a password.

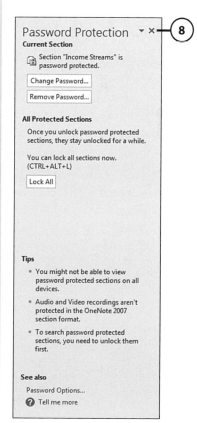

9. The next time you open the note-
    book and view the section, you
    are prompted for your password;
    type it in and click or tap OK to
    open the section.

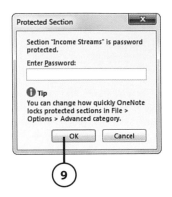

More Password Options

You can access additional
password options through
the OneNote Options dialog
box. Click or tap the Password
Options link at the bottom of the
Password Protection pane and
then scroll down to the Passwords
section to view settings.

Working with Pages and Subpages

You can use pages and subpages in your notebooks to further organize
notes. Pages are wide open—you can put whatever type of notes you want
on pages, including text, audio and video recordings, web pages, links,
pictures, and so on. Pages can hold a single note or many notes. You can also
create subpages, pages that are subordinate to the page above them in the
hierarchy display.

You can keep track of your pages by viewing the list of page tabs, the area at
the far right side of the OneNote program window. Just like sections, you can
give your pages distinct names. Page names appear at the top of the page
and in the page tabs list. You can use the page tabs list to navigate between
pages and subpages.

Add a Page

When you add a page with the Add Page command, OneNote places the new page at the end of the current section you're viewing.

1. Click or tap Add Page.

2. OneNote immediately adds an untitled page to the section.

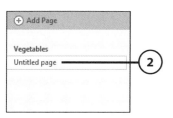

New Page Shortcuts

Another way to insert a new page is to right-click or press and hold a page tab and choose New Page. You can also press Ctrl+N on the keyboard.

Change the Page Name

You can assign unique names to the pages you add to a notebook. Page names appear as titles at the top of the page as well as on the page tabs.

1. Click or tap the page title area at the top of the page.

2. Type a name for the page and press Enter/Return.

3. OneNote assigns the page name to the title area and to the page's tab.

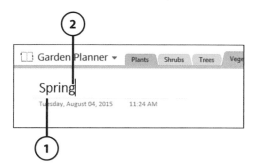

Naming Alternatives

You can right-click or press and hold a page tab to display a shortcut menu; then click or tap Rename. Type in a new name for the page and press Enter/Return.

>>>*Go Further*

CHANGE THE DATE OR TIME

OneNote inserts the current date and time below the newly created page title. You can edit the date or time setting, if needed. To edit the date, click or tap the date and click or tap the Change the Page Date icon (looks like a tiny calendar) and choose another date. To edit the time, click or tap the time and click or tap the Change the Page Time icon (looks like a tiny clock) to set another time.

Move a Page

You can move pages around to change their order of appearance in the page tabs listing or you can move them to other sections.

1. Drag the page tab and drop it on the section tab in which you want it to appear or drop it in the page tab list where you want it inserted.

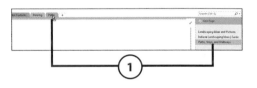

2. OneNote moves the page.

Moving Pages to Another Notebook

You can use the Move or Copy command to move a page to another notebook. Right-click or press and hold the page tab and choose Move or Copy. Next, click or tap the notebook you want to move to and click Move.

Delete a Page

You can remove a page you no longer want in a section. Pages you discard are placed in the notebook's Notebook Recycle Bin and kept for up to 60 days just in case you need to retrieve something you accidentally deleted.

1. Right-click or press and hold the page tab.

2. Click or tap Delete. OneNote immediately removes the page and places it in the notebook's Notebook Recycle Bin.

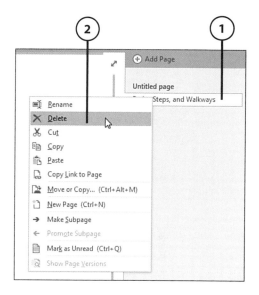

>>>Go Further

RESTORING A DELETED PAGE

OneNote keeps discarded pages and sections in the notebook's Notebook Recycle Bin, a special temporary holding area associated with the current notebook. If you find out you accidentally deleted a page you still need, you can recover it and move it back or copy it to another notebook entirely.

To recover a page from your notebook's Notebook Recycle Bin, click or tap the History tab, click or tap the Notebook Recycle Bin drop-down arrow, and then click the Notebook Recycle Bin command. This opens a special notebook of discarded sections and pages. Look for the page you want to restore listed in the Pages pane. Right-click the page tab and use the Move or Copy command to move the item back to the section where you want it to go. Pages kept in the Notebook Recycle Bin only stay there for 60 days. After that, they're deleted permanently. If you manually empty the Notebook Recycle Bin with the Empty Recycle Bin command, the pages are also permanently deleted.

Copy a Page

You can copy a page and place it in another section or another notebook.

1. Right-click or press and hold the page tab for the page you want to copy.

2. Click or tap Move or Copy.

3. Click or tap the notebook or section to which you want to copy the page.

4. Click or tap Copy and OneNote adds a copy of the page to the designated spot.

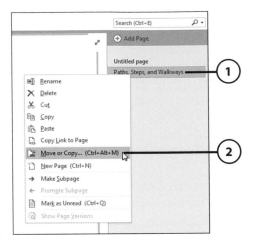

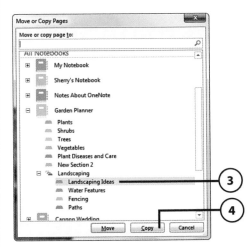

Make a Subpage

You can make a page subordinate to the page immediately above it. Subpages are another great way to organize notes. For example, if you're building a notebook around a class subject, you might create subpages for different semesters or terms. Subpages can be promoted or demoted.

1. Right-click or press and hold the page tab.

2. Click or tap Make Subpage.

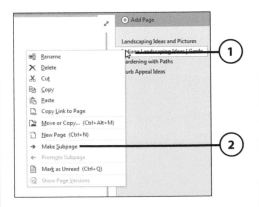

3. OneNote indents the page tab to indicate subpage status.

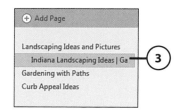

Drag It

Another way to make a subpage is to click and drag the page tab name in the Pages pane; drag the tab right to indent the page or drag left to promote the page.

Promote and Demote Subpages

OneNote lets you create two levels of subpages. For example, if you're using a notebook to assemble research for a scholastic paper, you might use pages and subpages to help you flesh out an outline and subject matter, organizing notes within each page. Subpage levels are noted by the amount of indentation in the page tab list.

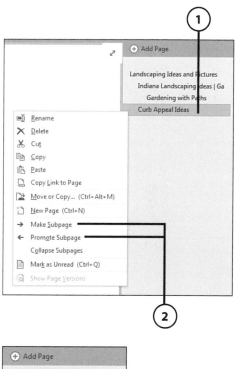

1. Right-click or press and hold the page tab.

2. Click or tap Promote Subpage to move the page up a level in the page hierarchy or Make Subpage to move the page down a level.

3. In this example, the subpage is demoted a second level.

>>>Go Further
USING ONENOTE FOR CREATING OUTLINES

If your OneNote project happens to revolve around research for a paper, there are a couple of ways you can build outlines in a notebook. One way is to use pages and subpages in your notebook to assist you with outlining your work. Pages and subpages in the Pages pane are arranged just like an outline, and you can promote or demote pages to change their positioning in the hierarchical structure.

You can also use the Increase Indent Position and Decrease Indent Position buttons on the Home tab for structuring an outline in a note. Lastly, the Numbering button, also located on the Home tab, is great for creating a specific type of outline format, such as Roman numerals or letters.

Expand and Collapse Subpages

You can collapse subpages as you work, much like you do when creating an outline in a word processing program. Collapsing subpages keeps them out of view so you can concentrate on other pages. You can expand subpages again to view the hierarchy. Collapsed pages are indicated by a downward-pointing arrow icon.

1. Right-click or press and hold the subpages' page tab.

2. To collapse the subpages, click or tap Collapse Subpages.

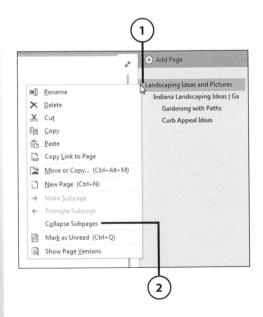

3. To expand subpages again, right-click or press and hold the page tab.

4. Click or tap Expand Subpages.

Collapse and Expand Shortcut

You can also click or tap the downward-pointing arrow icon next to the right of the page tab to expand or collapse subpages.

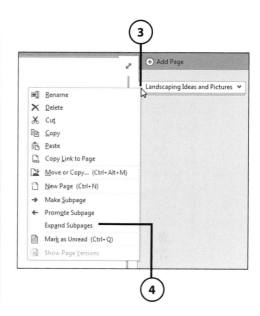

Using Page Templates

OneNote has a large variety of page templates you can use with your notebooks. Page templates offer preset layouts and formatting to help you create better, more uniform notes. Page templates can give your notes a more cohesive appearance and background. You can choose from five template categories, each with unique styles and designs. For example, the Academic category offers templates for classroom note-taking tasks, and the Decorative category includes stylized artwork to make your note pages more attractive. Many of the templates include preset content, called placeholder text; all you have to do is add your own text to start building notes. For example, the Simple Meeting Notes template offers preset text lists you can build on for recording meeting agenda notes, attendees list, and action items. Just click or tap the list and start typing to insert your own list notes.

Meeting Notes template   **Templates pane**

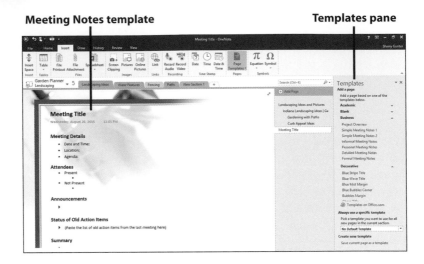

OneNote's page templates can be applied only to new pages or pages without any existing content. OneNote lets you modify a page template to create your own new template and save it to reuse it for other notebooks. For example, if you're using the Meeting Notes template and you don't need an attendees list, you can remove it from the page. You can also look for more templates from the Microsoft Office website (Office.com). New templates are featured and added all the time by users just like you.

Add a Page Based on a Template

You can use the Templates pane to choose from a library of page templates.

1. Click or tap Insert.

2. Click or tap the Page Templates button.

3. Click or tap the Page Templates command.

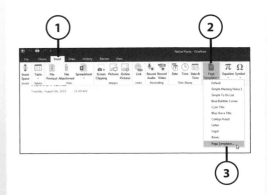

4. From the Templates pane, click or tap a category to expand its list of templates.

5. Click or tap a template to create a new page based on the design.

6. Click or tap the Close button to exit the Templates pane.

Page Templates Menu

OneNote keeps a list of recently applied templates and displays them whenever you click or tap the Page Templates button on the Insert tab. This makes it easy to reapply a favorite template again whenever you create a new page. The first time you click or tap the Page Templates button, no templates are listed.

Make It the Default Template

If you plan on using the same template over and over again, you can assign it as the default for every new page you create in a section. At the bottom of the Templates pane, click or tap the drop-down arrow and select your template from the list.

Go Online

To look for more templates, click or tap the Templates on Office.com link on the Templates task pane. This opens your default browser window to the Templates and Themes for Office Online web page. From here you can peruse a vast assortment of templates for all the Microsoft Office programs, including OneNote.

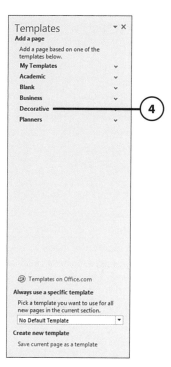

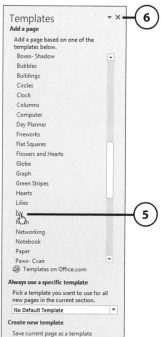

Create Your Own Template

OneNote lets you create your own templates to use with notebooks. You can make changes to an existing template or build your own template from scratch. In either case, you can save the page as a template file to reuse later.

1. After designing the page just the way you want it, open the Templates pane. (From the Insert tab, click or tap Page Templates and choose the Page Templates command.)

2. Click or tap Save Current Page as a Template.

3. Type a unique name for the new template file.

4. Optionally, if you want all new pages to use the new design, click or tap the Set as Default Template for New Pages in the Current Section check box.

5. Click or tap Save. OneNote adds this new template to the list of available templates found in the My Templates category on the Templates pane.

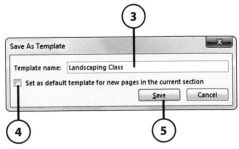

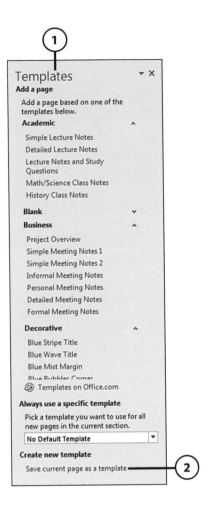

Change the Page Color

Rather than assigning a template design to a page, you can also simply change the page's background color. Normally, OneNote assigns a plain, white background, but you can choose another suitable color from the color palette menu. Much like changing section tab colors can help you quickly discern note content, changing page colors can help you visually organize notes, too.

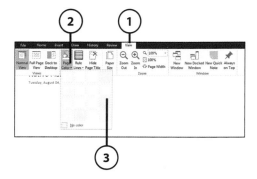

1. Click or tap View.

2. Click or tap Page Color.

3. Click or tap a color from the palette menu.

4. OneNote assigns the color to the page.

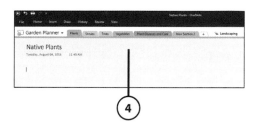

Color Variations
Page color may not apply to all parts of any template you previously assigned to the page.

It's Not All Good

Change It Back

If you don't like the page color you assigned, you can return it to the No Color default. Just click or tap No Color from the color palette menu to turn off the background color.

Notes are anything you place on a notebook page, including text, pictures, links, and drawings.

You can format note text.

File attachment

Picture as a note

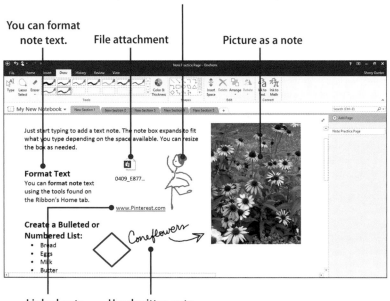

Linked note

Handwritten note

This chapter teaches you several different ways to add notes to your notebooks. Topics include

→ Typing in text notes

→ Formatting text notes to look nice

→ Creating bulleted and numbered lists

→ Handwriting notes with a stylus

→ Adding pictures as notes

→ Arranging notes on your notebook pages

Taking Notes

How do you like to take notes? Do you prefer typing in notes during a lecture or meeting using your laptop? Or perhaps you're a note-taker on the go with your smartphone, tapping in notes or drawing them on a touchscreen with a stylus? Do you like to record notes and review them later? Or maybe you prefer assembling notes based on web clippings and links to resources? No matter how you prefer to take notes, OneNote has all the note entry features you could possibly want.

Notes can be anything—simple lists, lengthy text, entire web pages, articles, drawings, pictures, random thoughts, scribbles, diagrams, charts, documents, or audio and video clips. Almost anything can be a note in OneNote based on how you want to use your notebook. If you're making a notebook for a classroom situation, your notes might be lecture recordings along with text notations. If you're creating a work-based notebook, your notes might be memos, meeting notes, charts, or graphs. If you're building a project notebook, the notes might be web clippings, pictures, budget tables, and To Do lists. In this chapter, you learn how easy it is to start adding notes to your pages.

Exploring Various Ways to Take Notes

You can start a new note anywhere on a page in your notebook. Notes appear in their own "boxes" on the screen when selected. The boxes simply act as containers for any type of note item you add, whether it's text, a picture, or a video clip. Of course you're not just limited to notes you type in yourself. You can also copy and paste data from other sources and insert it as notes. Notes can be just about anything.

For simplicity's sake, let's break down notes into several key categories:

Text-based   Notes you type in using the keyboard.

Pictures   Images, photos, graphics, or any kind of digital artwork can be inserted onto a page.

Files   Add a file to a notebook either as a page to itself or an attachment that you can open.

Links   Insert links to websites or to other notebooks or files on your computer.

Tables and spreadsheets   You can add a table to a page and use its column and row structure to organize information. You can also create an Excel spreadsheet or insert an existing spreadsheet.

Drawings   Make your own drawings using the Draw tools, including shapes and freehand drawings.

Handwriting   Using a touchscreen computer or device, you can hand write your notes using your finger or a stylus.

Audio and video recordings   Record audio and video clips as notes and use playback controls to hear or view content.

Text–based notes are easy to add. Just start typing anywhere on the page. The note container automatically expands to fit your note text. You can type in text just like you do in a word processing program; press Enter/Return to start a new paragraph, use the Tab key to indent text, and apply your favorite formatting commands. You can also select text to apply commands and features, such as selecting a word to make it bold or italicized. Text-based notes can be anything from a single word to a long document.

You can type directly on a page to create a text note.｜ ——— **Text note**

You can use the Insert tab on the Ribbon to add pictures as notes. Pictures can be photos, drawings, graphics, and so on. You can use the commands found on the Insert tab to insert screen clippings (pictures of what's on your computer screen), pictures (image files on your computer or digital camera), and online pictures (images you find on the Internet). Once you've placed an image on a page, you can resize it and move it around.

—— **Picture**

Do you want to insert an entire file as a note? You can add a file as a file attachment, which you can click or tap to view the contents, or you can add an entire file as a page in your notebook. Depending on the file size, the file may be added as multiple pages in a notebook section. (Learn more about file attachments in Chapter 5, "Using Note Features.")

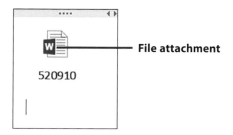

520910 —— **File attachment**

Links are an important part of note-taking, too. You can insert links to websites as well as to other files on your computer. OneNote underlines live links with a blue, clickable underline. When you click a link, your default web browser window opens to the site. Links are also created when you copy and paste an item from a website onto a notebook page.

Link

If you need to create tables, OneNote has two great features for building columns and rows: tables or spreadsheets. The Table command lets you draw a table any size using the number of columns and rows you specify and you can populate the table with whatever you want (text, pictures, links, and so on). The table's cells (the intersection of columns and rows) expand to fit whatever you put into them. If you want to use columns and rows to do a little number juggling, the Excel Spreadsheet command can help you out. You can build your own spreadsheet or insert an existing Excel spreadsheet. The nice thing about a spreadsheet is you can utilize all the wonderful tools associated with Excel to work with its data, including formulas and functions. In other words, you're embedding a fully functioning Excel spreadsheet. If you have any experience working with Microsoft Excel, you'll enjoy this feature.

Table

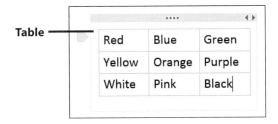

Red	Blue	Green
Yellow	Orange	Purple
White	Pink	Black

The occasion may arise in which you need to add your own drawings as notes. OneNote's drawing tools let you draw freehand or use preset shapes to create drawings. If you're using a touchscreen device, you can draw directly onto the screen or use a stylus. If you're a mouse user, you can draw with a mouse. The drawing tools in OneNote are similar to those found in the other Microsoft Office programs. You can layer objects, rotate them, change color and thickness, and more.

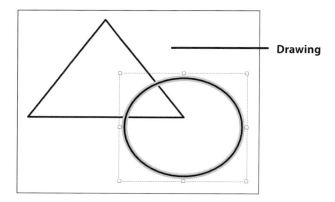

Drawing

OneNote recognizes your handwriting as note text. You can write notes with the Pen tool and control line thickness and color, or turn it into a highlighter. You can write on a touchscreen computer or device with a stylus, or just your finger. You can also quickly convert your handwritten notes into text notes using OneNote's Ink to Text feature. Plus, thanks to built-in OCR capabilities (Optical Character Recognition), OneNote can also now search for text within any images you save as notes.

Handwriting

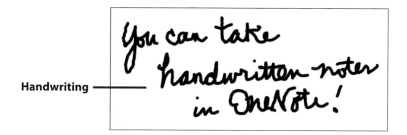

Finally, you can record audio and video as notes. With the Record Audio and Record Video commands, and a camera and microphone on your computer or device, you can record lectures, meetings, demos, music, and anything else you need to capture as a note. OneNote has built-in playback controls you can use to view or listen to your clips. Audio clips appear with a music note icon, while video clips appear with a filmstrip icon.

Audio note   **Video note**

Audio
Recording...

Audio recording started: 1:33 AM Friday, August 21, 2015

Video
Recording...

Video recording started: 1:35 AM Friday, August 21, 2015

In the remainder of this chapter, you learn how to add text notes, handwritten notes, and pictures. In the chapters to follow, you learn how to draw your own notes, insert tables and spreadsheets, add link notes, and record audio and video notes.

Typing Notes

Text notes are anything you type in using a keyboard. You can add a typed note anywhere on a page. Once you type in a note, you can apply a variety of formatting options. For example, you can make text bold, increase the font size, change the text color, change text positioning in the note box, and much more. In fact, just about all the formatting options you use in word processing programs (such as Microsoft Word) are available in OneNote.

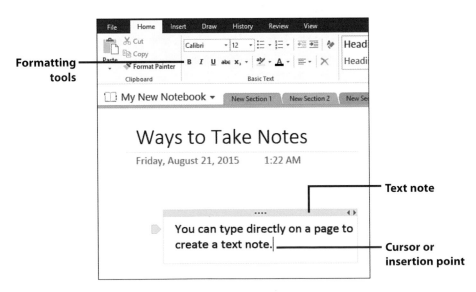

Formatting tools

Text note

Cursor or insertion point

Formatting controls are located on the Ribbon's Home tab, as well as a pop-up toolbar (called the Mini toolbar) that appears when you select text. To apply a formatting option, simply select the text you want to edit and choose a tool. Formatting is a great way to make your note text look better, especially if you're sharing notebooks with others. Formatting can also help you make your own notes appear more legible and easier to read.

Type a Note

Adding a text note is easy. All you have to do is pick a place on the page to start typing. A blinking vertical line, called a cursor or insertion point, marks your spot on the page as you type.

1. Click or tap on the page where you want the note to appear.

2. Type in your note text.

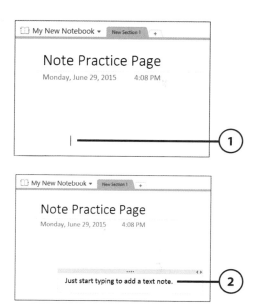

>>>*Go Further*

USING EDITING ACTIONS

Since text notes work just like any text entry task used in other programs, you can expect to use the same editing actions to make changes to text notes. The cursor always marks your spot as you type and you can click or tap in a word or sentence to move the cursor to another spot.

You can press the Backspace key to delete characters to the left of the cursor's location, for example, or press Delete to remove characters to the right of the cursor. You can also use the keyboard's arrow keys to move the cursor around a note text box. The Home key, when pressed, takes you to the front of a line of text and the End key takes you to the end of the line. Pressing Enter/Return starts a new paragraph. If you want extra space between paragraphs, press Enter/Return twice.

Selecting text works the same way, too. Double-click to select a word; triple-click to select a paragraph. Click or tap the note box border to select the entire note.

Apply Basic Formatting

You can choose from a variety of formatting options for your note text. You can apply basic formatting commands, for example, such as bold, italics, and underlining, or assign a different font and font size. Formatting commands are located on the Ribbon's Home tab.

1. Select the text or note you want to edit. Drag across the word(s) to highlight the selection.

2. Click or tap the Home tab.

3. To apply bold, italics, or underlining, click or tap a button.

4. OneNote applies the formatting to the selected text; in this example, bold is applied.

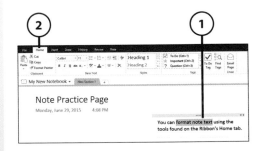

You can format note text using the tools found on the Ribbon's Home tab.

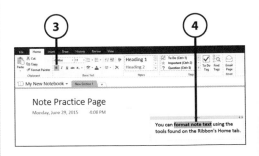

You can format note text using the tools found on the Ribbon's Home tab.

Use the Mini Toolbar

Whenever you select note text, the Mini toolbar pops up, offering shortcuts to formatting commands. You can click or tap a button on the Mini toolbar to quickly apply a command, such as clicking the Bold button to apply bold. Learn more about using the Mini toolbar in Chapter 1, "Getting Started with OneNote."

5. To change the font, click or tap the Font drop-down arrow and choose another font from the menu list.

6. The font is applied to the selected text.

7. To change the font size, click or tap the Font Size drop-down arrow and choose another size from the list.

8. The selected text displays the new font size.

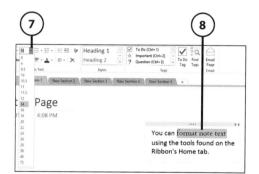

Pin It

If you plan on applying a lot of formatting to your note text, consider pinning the Home tab in place so you don't have to keep opening it. With the Home tab displayed, click or tap the Pin the Ribbon icon located in the far right-hand corner of the Ribbon. The icon looks like a pushpin. To unpin the Ribbon later, click or tap the Collapse the Ribbon icon, which replaces the Pin the Ribbon icon display.

Using Strikethrough, Subscript, and Superscript

Though not really considered basic formatting, the Strikethrough, Subscript, and Superscript tools are also found in the Basic Text formatting group on the Home tab. Strikethrough puts a line through the text like a proofreader's deletion mark (~~example~~). Subscript and superscript make the text smaller in size and set it below or above the text baseline, respectively. You might use a subscript to write a chemical compound (H_2O) or superscript for a mathematical expression (42^2). Both superscript and subscript are found on the same button on the Home tab; click or tap the button's drop-down arrow to switch between the two settings.

Apply Bullets and Numbers

To make your note lists and step text easy to read, you can apply bullets and numbers.

1. Select the text or note you want to edit.

2. Click or tap the Ribbon's Home tab.

3. To apply bullets, click or tap the Bullets drop-down arrow.

4. Click or tap a bullet style.

5. Bullets are added to the selected text.

Quick Click Method

If you prefer to use the default bullet style, just click or tap the Bullets button and not the drop-down arrow next to it. In the same manner, to use the default number style, click or tap the Numbering button. Both commands remember the last bullet or number style you applied and it's ready to reuse with a click or tap of the button.

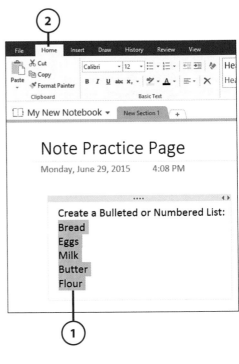

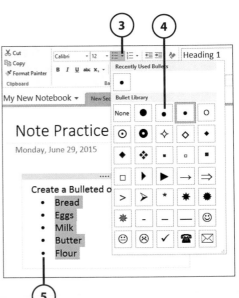

6. To create a numbered list, click or tap the Numbering drop-down arrow.

7. Click or tap a number style.

8. Numbers are immediately applied to the selected text.

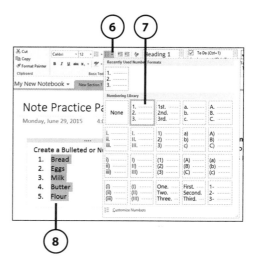

Bullets on the Fly

You can continue a bulleted or numbered list without having to reapply more bullets or numbers formatting. OneNote keeps the designated formatting going as you add new lines of text to the list. To end the list formatting, press Enter/Return twice at the end of the list.

Change Text Alignment

You can control the positioning of text within a note using the alignment commands. You can align the text to the left of the box, to the right, or center the text.

1. Select the text or note you want to edit.

2. Click or tap the Home tab.

3. Click or tap the Paragraph Alignment button.

4. Click or tap an alignment from the list.

5. OneNote applies the alignment to the text.

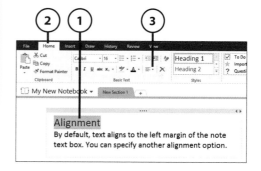

Alignment
By default, text aligns to the left margin of the note text box. You can specify another alignment option.

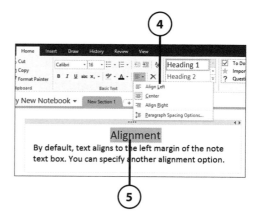

Alignment
By default, text aligns to the left margin of the note text box. You can specify another alignment option.

Control Paragraph Spacing

Use the Paragraph Spacing Options command at the bottom of the Paragraph Alignment menu list to open the Paragraph Spacing dialog box. You can specify how much space you want to include before and after paragraphs. When you apply these settings, they're applied to the currently selected text or paragraph.

Mini Toolbar

When you select note text, a pop-up toolbar, called the Mini toolbar, appears offering you quick access to the same formatting tools found on the Home tab. Just click or tap a command from the Mini toolbar to apply it.

Indent Text

You can apply the Increase Indent Position and Decrease Indent Position commands when you want to change the indentation of your paragraph text within the note box margins.

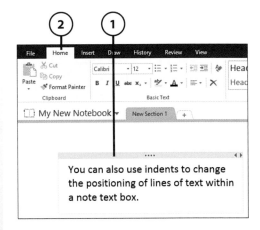

You can also use indents to change the positioning of lines of text within a note text box.

1. Select the text or note you want to edit.

2. Click or tap the Home tab.

3. To increase the indent, click or tap Increase Indent Position.

4. The text indents within the note text box.

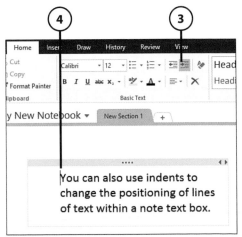

You can also use indents to change the positioning of lines of text within a note text box.

Quick Indent

Another quick way to create an instant indent is to press the Tab key on the keyboard. This creates an indent for the current line of text you're typing.

5. To decrease the indent again, click or tap Decrease Indent Position.

6. The indent is decreased in the note text box.

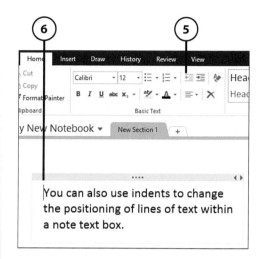

Change the Font Color

You can change the color of your text using the Font Color command. You can choose from a palette of colors. By default, note text is automatically black unless you've applied a theme to your page, in which case it might be another color.

1. Select the text or note you want to edit.

2. Click or tap the Home tab.

3. Click or tap the Font Color drop-down arrow.

4. Click or tap a color from the list.

5. The color is immediately applied to the note text.

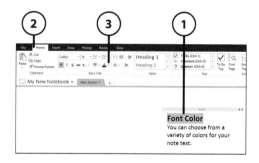

Font Color
You can choose from a variety of colors for your note text.

More Colors

If you click or tap the More Colors command at the bottom of the Font Color menu list, the Colors dialog box opens and you can choose from a wider variety of color choices.

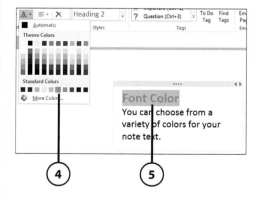

Font Color
You can choose from a variety of colors for your note text.

Copying Formatting

Rather than tediously format each note box separately, you can use the Format Painter tool to reapply all the same formatting quickly and easily. Start by selecting the text containing the formatting you want to copy. Next, click or tap the Format Painter tool on the Home tab and then drag across the text you want to apply the formatting to; OneNote immediately applies the copied formatting.

Apply a Style

Borrowing from Microsoft Word, you can apply a few select styles in OneNote. Styles are preset formatting you can use to give your note text a uniform look throughout the notebook. For example, you can apply the Heading 1 style to note titles, or a Citation style to mark citation text differently on a page.

1. Select the text or note you want to edit, or simply click or tap anywhere within the text.

2. Click or tap the Home tab.

3. Click or tap the More button in the Styles gallery box.

4. Click or tap a style from the menu.

5. The style is applied to the selected text.

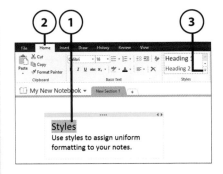

Styles
Use styles to assign uniform formatting to your notes.

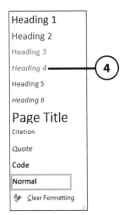

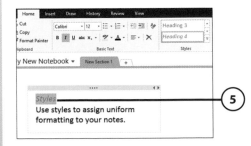

Styles
Use styles to assign uniform formatting to your notes.

It's Not All Good

Style Limitations

Unlike in Word, you cannot modify styles or create new styles. The gallery list of available styles is limited to a few common heading styles and styles for research, such as Citation or Quote.

Remove All Formatting

If you don't like the styles or formatting you've applied, you can clear it from the text using the Clear All Formatting tool. This tool removes all the formatting you have applied, including styles and font changes, and leaves the text plain again.

1. Select the text or note you want to edit.

2. Click or tap the Home tab.

3. Click or tap the Clear All Formatting.

4. All formatting is removed from the selected text.

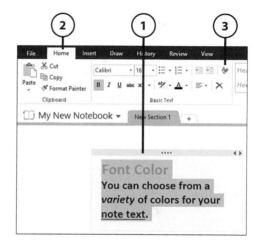

Undo and Redo

Don't forget about the handy Undo and Redo commands. Undo undoes your last edit, while Redo reapplies the edit again. Look for both commands in OneNote's Quick Access toolbar. You can also use keyboard shortcuts to activate the commands; press Ctrl+Z for Undo, or Ctrl+Y for Redo.

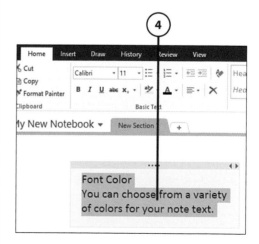

Handwriting Notes

You can write out your note text by hand if you're using a touchscreen computer or device. You can write with your finger or a stylus. Handwritten notes, like text notes, can be placed anywhere on the page. Handwriting your notes comes in handy if you need to take notes but do not want the sound of tapping on a keyboard, such as when in a meeting or in a classroom. OneNote's drawing tools are also a great way to annotate notes, pictures, screenshots, charts, and other elements you add to a page.

Draw tab **Pen tool selection** **Handwritten note text**

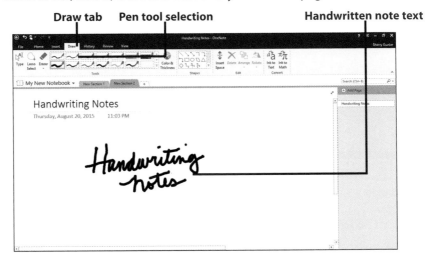

Mind you, not everyone's handwriting is legible on a touchscreen. It's never quite as smooth and neat as pen on paper, but OneNote does its best to recognize your scrawls. You can even turn your handwriting into typed text using OneNote's Convert to Text tool.

All the drawing tools, including the Pen tool you select for writing onscreen, are located on the Ribbon's Draw tab. Open the tab to view a gallery of pen styles and colors. You can even apply a highlighter effect for your pen and highlight other notes on the page. If you don't see the line thickness or color you want to use, you can open the Color & Thickness dialog box and fine-tune your instrument.

Unlike the pen and paper scenario, when you draw on a computer screen, you're using pixels. Pixels aren't round and smooth, they're square and raggedy. For that reason, you may find your handwriting onscreen improves if you make adjustments to the line thickness of the Pen tool. For example, if you choose a thicker Pen setting, cursive writing may appear more legible.

Thinner line   Thicker line

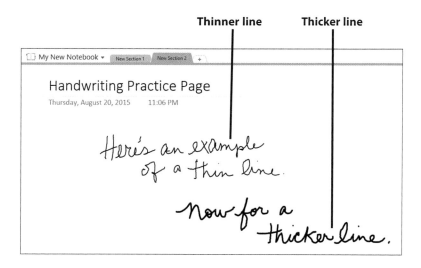

Add a Handwritten Note

You can use a stylus or your finger to handwrite a note directly onto a touchscreen. OneNote's Pen tool lets you write anywhere and you can choose an ink color and line thickness.

1. Click or tap the Draw tab.

2. Click or tap the pen style you want to use.

3. To change the line thickness or color, click or tap the Color & Thickness button.

4. With the Pen option selected, click or tap a line thickness.

5. Optionally, click or tap a color.

6. Click or tap OK.

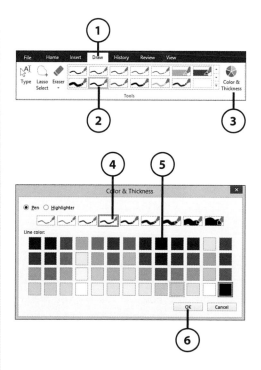

7. Start writing on the screen using your finger or a stylus.

8. On the Draw tab, click or tap Type to return to a regular mouse pointer onscreen.

Drawing Other Things

You can also use the Pen tool to draw other things onscreen, such as shapes, freeform illustrations, and more. Learn how to use the Drawing tools in Chapter 7, "Drawing Notes."

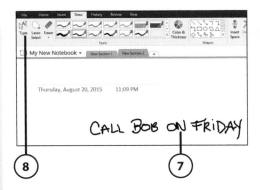

Erase Your Writing

You can erase your handwriting using the Eraser tool. Much like an eraser works to clear a chalkboard, you can use the Eraser tool to wipe away all or part of things you draw onscreen, including handwriting. The Eraser tool removes only drawn items; text notes are not affected by the erasing process. You can choose from several different eraser sizes, including the Stroke Eraser for removing a single stroke of your handwriting. The Eraser tool toggles on or off with each click of the button.

1. Click or tap the Draw tab.

2. Click or tap the Eraser button's drop-down arrow.

3. Click or tap an eraser size.

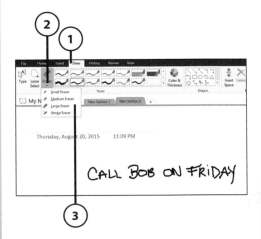

4. Drag across the handwriting you want to erase, or just click or tap on the writing. You may need to drag across several times or click or tap several sections to delete them all.

5. OneNote removes the drawing.

6. Click or tap the Eraser button on the Draw tab to turn the tool off again.

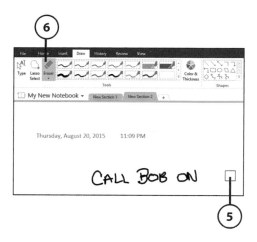

Undo

You can also use the Undo command to quickly undo an erasure. Click or tap the Undo button on the Quick Access toolbar, or press Ctrl+Z on the keyboard.

Select Handwritten Text

If you need to move a handwritten note, you must first select it. You can use Type mode to drag a box around the text to select it.

1. From the Draw tab, click or tap Type.

2. Starting with the top-left corner, drag across the writing until everything you want to select is included in the box.

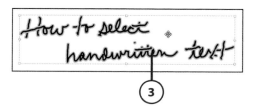

3. OneNote instantly selects all of the handwriting and surrounds the writing with a box that you can then move, resize, or even delete.

Convert a Handwritten Note into Text

OneNote's Ink to Text tool can turn your handwritten notes into text notes that look just like you typed them in.

1. Select the handwriting you want to convert.

2. From the Draw tab, click or tap Ink to Text.

3. OneNote converts the handwriting to a typed note.

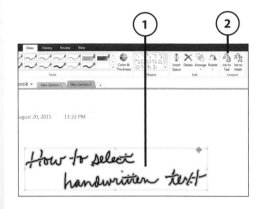

Multiple Language Support

OneNote supports multiple languages, such as Chinese, German, French, Korean, and Spanish. If you handwrite your notes in a supported language, OneNote can convert it to editable text.

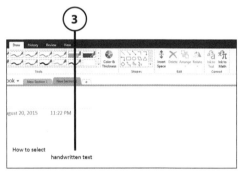

It's Not All Good

Handwriting Recognition Problems?

OneNote does a pretty good job of recognizing your handwriting to convert to typed text. Anything resembling "text" can be converted. However, it's possible OneNote might not pick up on all the letters you scrawl onscreen. In this case, you can try selecting the missed writing using the Lasso tool on the Draw tab. Once you've selected the text, right-click the selection and choose Treat Selected Ink As, and then choose Handwriting. If this doesn't work, you might have to type in the text manually.

Adding Pictures

OneNote makes it easy to add pictures to your notebooks. Depending on the type of notebook you're building, pictures can be every bit as important as text notes. You can even create a notebook that functions as a picture album! You can add pictures to your notebooks in three main ways: Insert a picture file found on your computer, insert a picture you find on the Internet, or take a picture of what's on your screen (called a *screen clipping*).

Any picture files you store on your computer, such as photos from your digital camera or photos you scan, can be inserted onto a notebook page. Image files come in a variety of formats, and OneNote supports most of them. If you use a digital camera, you can also download pictures into OneNote. Whether you call them pictures, photos, or images, you can add them to OneNote.

Picture tools   Selection box

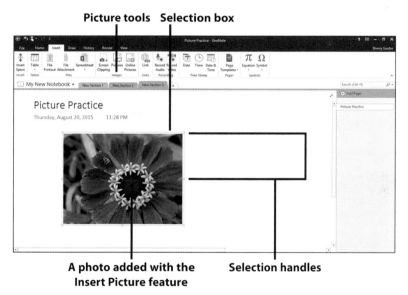

**A photo added with the   Selection handles
Insert Picture feature**

You can also insert pictures you find on the Web, called *online pictures* in OneNote. The Insert Pictures dialog box lets you use pictures from Bing search results, your OneDrive cloud storage, or from sites like Facebook or Flickr. When using Bing Image Search, keep in mind that many of the photos you find on the Web are licensed; this means you must follow copyright laws where applicable.

OneNote's Screen Clipping tool takes a picture of what's on your computer or device screen and inserts it as an image. You simply select an area of the screen, such as a dialog box, or the entire screen, and OneNote takes a snapshot of the screen.

Pictures are treated just like any other note. Pictures are contained in their own note boxes, which can be moved, resized, copied, pasted, and more. When you select a picture, a box that has selection handles surrounds it. You can use the handles to resize the picture, or drag the box border to move the picture.

Insert a Picture

Use the Insert Picture dialog box to add a picture from your computer or camera.

1. Click or tap where you want to insert the picture.

2. Click or tap the Insert tab.

3. Click or tap Pictures.

4. The Insert Picture dialog box opens; navigate to the folder or drive containing the picture file you want to insert.

5. Click or tap the picture filename.

6. Click or tap Insert.

7. OneNote adds the picture.

Copy and Paste

You can also copy and paste a picture. Simply copy the picture from its original location (press Ctrl+C on the keyboard) and then paste it onto a notebook page (press Ctrl+V on the keyboard).

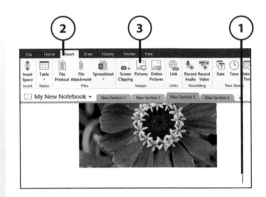

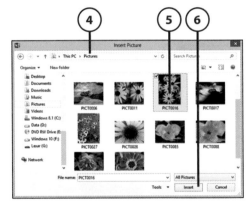

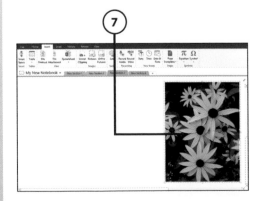

Add a Picture from OneDrive

If you use the OneDrive cloud storage, you can select pictures you store on your account and insert them into a notebook.

1. Click or tap where you want to insert the picture.

2. Click or tap the Insert tab.

3. Click or tap Online Pictures.

4. The Insert Pictures dialog box opens; click or tap the OneDrive Browse link.

5. A list of your stored pictures appears; click or tap the picture you want to use.

6. Click or tap Insert.

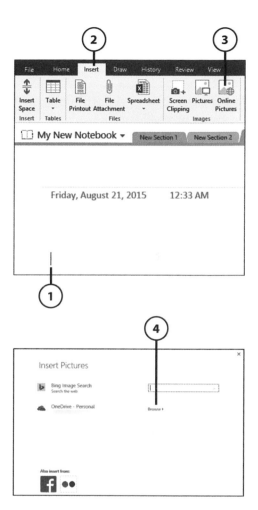

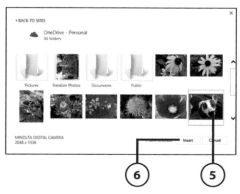

7. The file is downloaded and inserted onto the page.

Need a OneDrive Account?

OneDrive cloud storage is free with any Microsoft account. You can use your OneDrive storage to store up to 15GB of data, including all kinds of files. To learn more about using OneDrive with OneNote, see Chapter 14, "Taking OneNote Online."

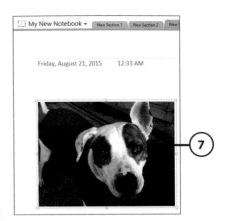

Add a Picture with Bing Search

You can use the Bing Image Search service to find a picture online to insert into a notebook.

1. Click or tap where you want to insert the picture.

2. Click or tap the Insert tab.

3. Click or tap Online Pictures.

4. Type in a keyword or phrase for the type of picture you're looking for.

5. Click or tap Search or press Enter/Return.

6. A list of search results appears; click the Close button to close the disclaimer box.

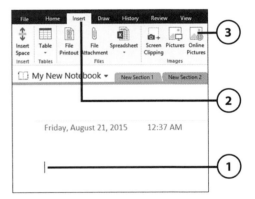

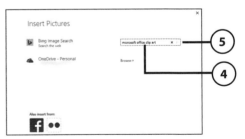

7. Scroll through the pictures and click or tap the picture you want to use.

8. Click or tap Insert.

9. The file is downloaded and inserted onto the page.

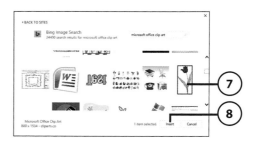

Delete It

If you don't like the picture you insert, you can always delete it. Click or tap the picture to select it and press Delete on the keyboard.

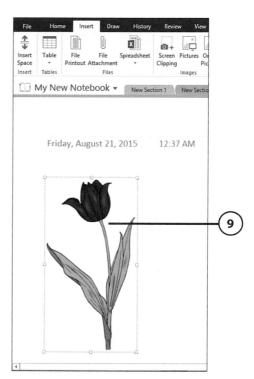

Add a Picture from Facebook

You can connect Microsoft Office to your Facebook account and use pictures you store on Facebook.com. When you set up this feature, the Facebook option is added to the list of online services to choose from. These steps demonstrate how to add the service and insert a Facebook picture.

1. Click or tap the Insert tab.

2. Click or tap Online Pictures.

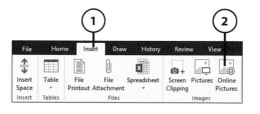

3. Click or tap the Facebook icon. (If Facebook is already an option listed, you can skip to step 11.)

4. Click Connect.

5. Type in the email account associated with Facebook.

6. Type in your Facebook password.

7. Click or tap Log In.

8. Click or tap Okay.

9. Click or tap Done.

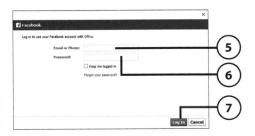

10. The Facebook service is added to the list of online picture sites.

11. To add a picture from Facebook, click or tap See More.

12. Click or tap the picture you want to insert.

13. Click or tap Insert.

14. The picture is added to the notebook page.

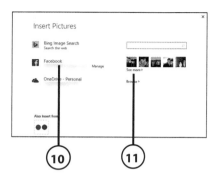

Flickr, Too!

You can follow similar steps to add your Flickr photo account to the list of online services shown in the Insert Pictures dialog box. Simply click or tap the Flickr icon to set up the account to work with Microsoft OneNote.

Insert Screen Clippings

You can use the Screen Clipping feature to capture a picture of your computer or device screen and insert it onto a notebook page. As soon as you activate the tool, the OneNote window is immediately minimized and the capture is ready to go. For that reason, you may need to do a little setup work first before taking a snapshot. Open the program or browser window you want to capture before actually activating the command.

1. Click or tap where you want to insert the clipping.

2. Click or tap the Insert tab.

3. Click or tap Screen Clipping.

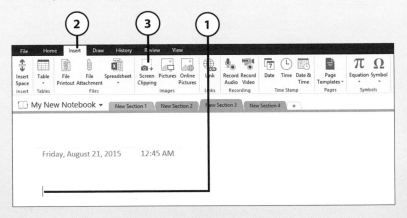

4. Drag across the area of the screen you want to capture.

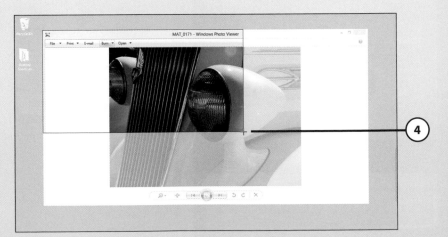

5. OneNote inserts the clipping onto the page. You can resize or move the picture as needed.

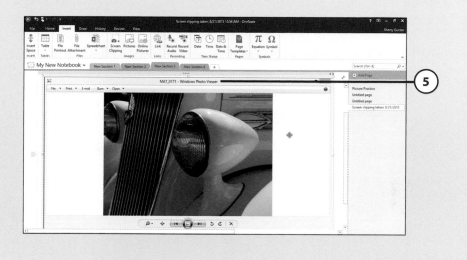

Arranging Notes

As you add more and more notes to a page, you may find yourself needing to do a little housekeeping to keep things looking nice. You can arrange your notes by moving them around, resizing them, and even inserting extra space between them to make things easy to read.

Move a Note

When you select a note, you'll notice a dashed border surrounds it. You can drag and drop the note anywhere you want it to go, including into another section or page.

1. Click or tap the note you want to move.

2. Hover the mouse pointer over the selected note until you see a four-sided arrow icon.

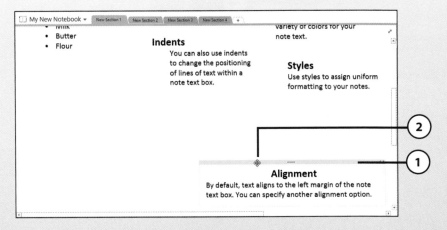

3. Drag and drop the note where you want it to go.

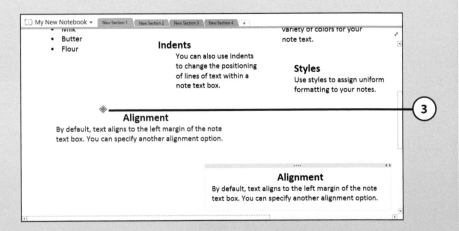

Resize a Note

It's easy to resize a note. You can do so using the note's selection handles—the tiny squares located at the corners or sides of the note selection box.

1. Click or tap the note you want to resize.

2. Move the mouse pointer over a selection handle; the mouse pointer becomes a two-sided arrow icon.

3. Drag the selection handle to resize the note. The note is resized depending on which direction you drag and which selection handle you choose.

Cut, Copy, and Paste a Note

The ever reliable Cut, Copy, and Paste commands can help you arrange note items on a page. You can use the Cut command to remove a note and paste it somewhere else, or not at all if you want to delete the note. You can use the Copy command to make a duplicate of the note and paste it somewhere else.

1. Click or tap the note.

2. Click or tap the Home tab.

3. To move the note, click or tap Cut; to copy the note, click or tap Copy.

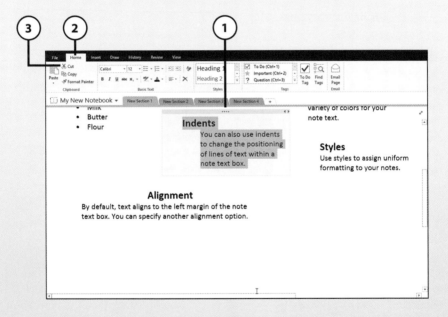

Using the Windows Clipboard

When you cut and copy notes, they're placed on the Windows Clipboard, a temporary behind-the-scenes storage area on your computer. An item you cut or copy is placed on the Clipboard until you paste it where you want it to go. Typically, the Clipboard only lets you paste the last item cut or copied. The item remains on the Clipboard until you cut or copy something else or until you turn off your computer or laptop.

4. Click or tap where you want to paste the note.

5. Click or tap Paste.

6. The note is pasted.

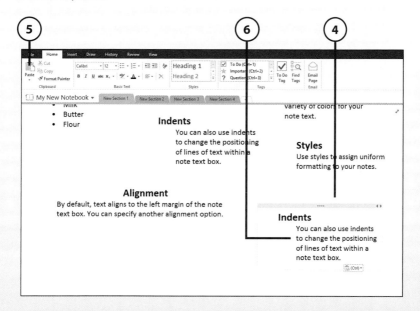

Keyboard Shortcuts

The keyboard shortcut keys for the Cut, Copy, and Paste commands are just about the same with every program these days. To apply the Cut command, press Ctrl+X. To copy, press Ctrl+C. To paste, press Ctrl+V.

Add Space Between Notes

When you find yourself needing some extra space between notes or you need to make room on the left margin, you can apply the Insert Space tool. When applied, notes move over based on where you want to add space. You can add space horizontally or vertically to a page. You can also use the feature to remove extra space on a page.

1.   Click or tap the Insert tab.

2.   Click or tap the Insert Space command.

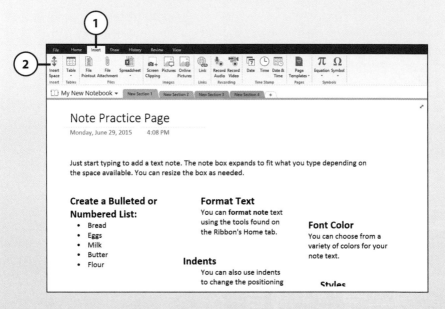

3.   Move the mouse pointer to the place on the page where you want to add space; a line appears either vertically or horizontally, depending on where you hover the mouse pointer.

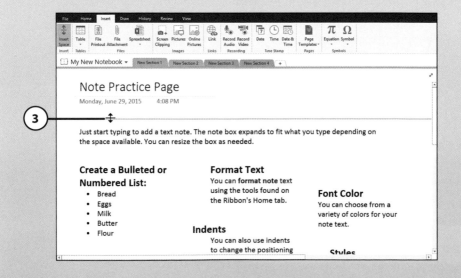

4. Click and drag the arrow to add the amount of space you need.

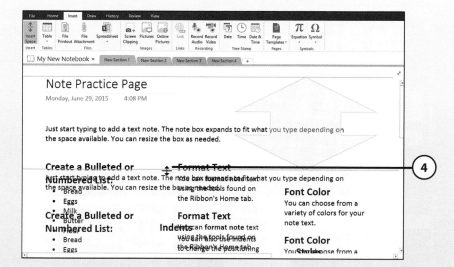

5. When you release the mouse button, the space is added to the page.

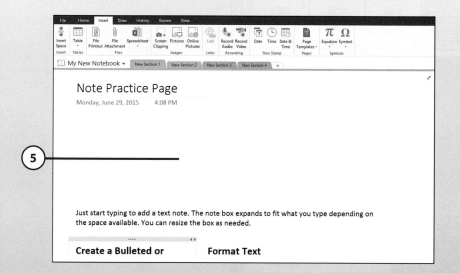

Undo It

If you don't like the spacing results, use the Undo command (press Ctrl+Z) to undo the space creation and try again.

Delete a Note

There are several ways to delete a note you no longer want to keep. You can use the Delete key on the keyboard, the Delete button on the Home tab, or the Delete command found on the shortcut menu. All three methods accomplish the same task—deleting the selected note. These steps show how to use the Delete command.

1. Click or tap the note you want to remove.

2. Click or tap the Home tab.

3. Click or tap Delete.

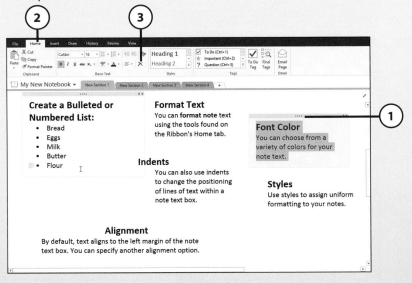

4. OneNote deletes the note.

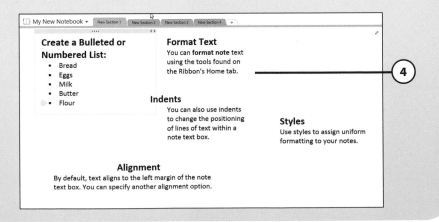

>>>*Go Further*

A WORD ABOUT DELETING

The Delete action, by its very name, conveys certain permanence. When you apply the Delete command, or any of its shortcuts, to delete a note, the note is permanently removed. Or is it? You can apply the Undo command (located on the Quick Access Toolbar) to undo the last few actions you performed, including deletions. For example, if one of your recent actions was to delete a note, clicking or tapping the Undo button can bring the note back again. In that same vein, the Redo command (also located on the Quick Access Toolbar) can be used to redo the actions again. Deleted notes are temporarily available to undo and redo as needed.

The Delete command you apply to remove notes works a little differently than the Delete command you apply to pages and sections in your notebook. As you learned in Chapter 3, "Working with Sections, Pages, and Subpages," discarded pages and sections are moved to the notebook's Notebook Recycle Bin. Operating much like the Windows Recycle Bin, deleted pages and sections are held there for up to 60 days (unless you permanently empty the bin before then). You can restore a discarded section or page, if needed.

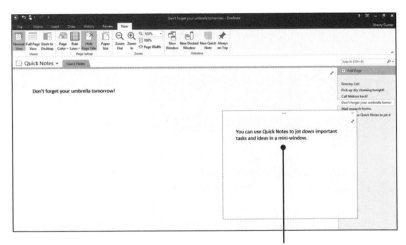

You can use Quick Notes to make
notes without a notebook.

In this chapter, you learn how to use some of OneNote's other note-taking features and tools. Topics include

→ Inserting date and time stamps into your notes
→ Writing mathematical expressions and equations as notes
→ Inserting entire files as notes
→ Embedding files as links
→ Clipping web content with the OneNote Clipper tool
→ Using Quick Notes to jot down quick notes

Using Note Features

You can find a variety of different features to help you work with notebooks and notes, ranging from marking notes with dates and times to capturing web content to turn into notes. You can use many of these additional features to improve how you work with OneNote and, in some cases, simplify your note-taking tasks. For example, you can use Quick Notes to jot down instant notes outside the OneNote program window, such as writing down a reminder note about making a phone call. Or you can use the Ink to Math feature to turn your written math equations into tidy typed equations anyone can legibly read.

In this chapter, you learn about several of these handy features and how they might work for you.

Inserting Date and Time Stamps

OneNote has several tools you can use to help you mark or track chronological notes. The date and time stamps mark a note with the current date or time, respectively. Let's say you're using a notebook to record your daily office tasks, such as sales calls you make, orders you receive, and so on. You may need to keep track of when each entry note in your notebook is added. Or perhaps you're using OneNote to keep a journal. The date and time stamps can help you mark each entry with the date and time it was created.

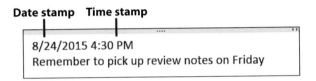

When you assign a date or time stamp, it's added wherever the cursor or insertion point is located in the note box. If you start a new note, the stamp is added at the top of the note. If you click somewhere in the middle of a text note, the time or date is added there. You can choose to add just the date, just the time, or both together.

Add a Date and Time Stamp

The Date and Time Stamp features add the current date or time to your note. Use this feature to keep track of when your notes were taken. You can add the time, the date, or both.

1. Click or tap where you want the date or time stamp added.

2. Click or tap Insert.

3. Next, you can click or tap the Date button, the Time button, or the Date & Time button.

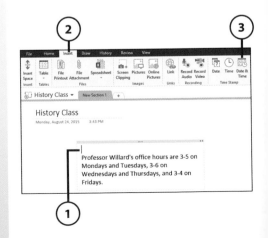

4. OneNote adds the stamp to the note. In this example, the Date & Time stamp is added.

8/24/2015 4:42 PM
Professor Willard's office hours are 3-5 on Mondays and Tuesdays, 3-6 on Wednesdays and Thursdays, and 3-4 on Fridays.

Editing the Date and Time

You can change the date or time stamp you added to a note. Click or tap the stamp and make your edits. Update the date or time by clicking or tapping the appropriate button again. To remove the stamp completely from your note, select the date or time and press Delete on the keyboard.

>>>Go Further

CONTROLLING THE DATE AND TIME

OneNote's date and time stamp information (the actual date and time) is controlled through your computer or device's date and time settings. For example, in Windows, you can adjust the computer's date and time settings using the time and date display on the taskbar. Click or tap the time and date to open the Date and Time Settings box displaying a calendar and clock. You can make adjustments, as needed, to the date or the time. You can also click or tap the Change date and time settings link if you need to change the time zone.

>>>Go Further

DEALING WITH PAGE STAMPS

You probably already noticed that OneNote automatically places a date and time stamp under the page title in your notebook. Every new page you add includes a date and time stamp marking its creation. You can change the date and time, if needed. If you click or tap the date, a tiny Calendar icon appears next to the selection. Click or tap the icon to open a monthly calendar. You can choose another date by clicking it on the calendar, and you can navigate between months to find just the right date you're looking for.

The page's time stamp works similarly. Click or tap the time stamp to display a tiny Clock icon. Click or tap the icon to open a Change Page Time dialog box. You can use the drop-down menu to set a different page time, and then click or tap OK to exit the dialog box and apply the change.

If you prefer not to include the date or time stamp on your page, you can delete both stamps entirely. Simply click or tap either stamp and press Delete. Once removed, they're gone for good.

Calculating with OneNote

Although it's not a spreadsheet program, you can perform simple math expressions and equations in OneNote. Perhaps you're sitting in a meeting and need to jot down some numbers and perform some quick calculations, or maybe you're working on a scientific project and want to write down some equations. OneNote can instantly calculate the results, and you can decide whether to keep the information in a note or discard it altogether.

Along with basic math (addition, subtraction, multiplication, and division), OneNote recognizes a few mathematical expressions, such as averaging, percentages, and exponentials. OneNote supports several basic trigonometry functions, too, such as calculating the square root (SQRT). You can quickly calculate SIN, COS, logarithms, radians, and more. Just remember to follow any function code with the number, angle, or variables surrounded in parentheses.

Type out your mathematical equations just like you would enter them into a calculator and OneNote's built-in feature figures out the results. For example, to divide 1000 by 25, you write out the equation like this:

1000/25=

OneNote also supports Greek symbols used in mathematics. To add them to an equation, use the Symbol drop-down list found on the Ribbon's Insert tab.

If you prefer writing out your math equations by hand, you can utilize OneNote's Ink to Math feature. A special editor window opens for you to handwrite your equation. OneNote recognizes your number scrawls and converts them for you to insert an equation in a note.

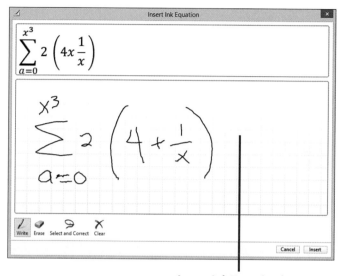

Insert Ink Equation box

OneNote also offers a library of preset equations and some powerful tools for customizing them. When you activate a preset equation, a new tab of equation design tools is added to the Ribbon.

In this section, you learn how to put the methods described to use to add calculations to your notes.

Type a Mathematical Expression

You can type equations and simple mathematical expressions and let OneNote's built-in features figure out the results.

1. Type out the mathematical expression or equation you want to calculate, ending with an equal sign (=).

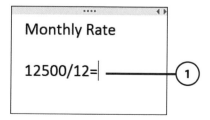

2. Press the Spacebar or Enter/
   Return on the keyboard.

3. The results immediately appear
   after the equal sign.

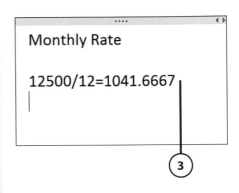

Arithmetic Operators

OneNote supports all the basic
mathematical operators: addition (+),
subtraction (-), multiplication (*), and
division (/). You can also calculate
percent (%), exponentiation (^), and
factorial computation (!).

Add a Symbol

If your mathematical equation
requires a Greek symbol, you can
insert one using the Symbol drop-
down menu list.

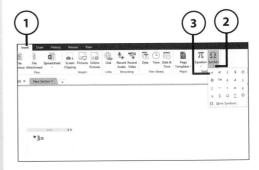

1. Click or tap Insert.

2. Click or tap the Symbol drop-
   down arrow.

3. Click or tap a symbol from the list.

4. OneNote automatically inserts it
   into your equation. In this example, the pi symbol is inserted.

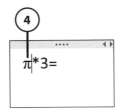

More Symbols

If you don't see your symbol listed in the
menu, you can open the Symbol dialog
box to look for it. The Symbol dialog box
includes currency symbols, Latin, super-
scripts and subscripts, and more. Click
the More Symbols option at the bottom
of the Symbol menu to open the dialog
box. Once open, choose the symbol you
want to use and click or tap Insert.

Turn a Handwritten Equation into Math

You can use the Insert Ink Equation feature to handwrite equations and turn them into typed equations. Touchscreen users can write with a stylus or draw with their finger directly onto the screen. If you don't have a touchscreen device, you can use the mouse to draw equations in the Insert Ink Equation box. The box you write in automatically expands to fit the symbols and numbers you add.

1. Click or tap Draw.

2. Click or tap Ink to Math.

3. Write out the equation you want to enter.

4. A preview of the typed equation appears here.

5. You can use the editing tools to make any corrections.

6. When the equation looks ready to add to your notes, click or tap Insert.

7. The equation is added as typed text and numbers.

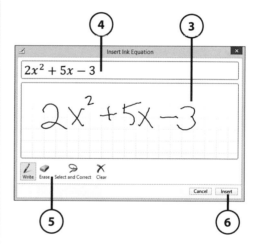

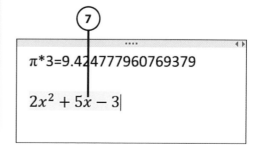

It's Not All Good

Practice Makes Perfect

The Insert Ink Equation editor tries its best to decipher your handwriting. It may take a few entries to get it right, though. If it doesn't recognize your writing at first, you can use the editing tools to make changes and try again. If you're having trouble with one particular symbol or number, click or tap the Select and Correct tool and drag a circle around the symbol or number. A pop-up list of possible matches appears and you can choose the correct one from the list.

Use Built-In Equations

You can drop in any of the built-in equations available in the Equation gallery and use them in your notes. When you do, a new tab of controls appears on the Ribbon. You can use the Equation Tools to customize and edit the elements of your equation.

1. Click or tap Insert.

2. Click or tap the Equation drop-down arrow.

3. Click or tap the equation you want to use.

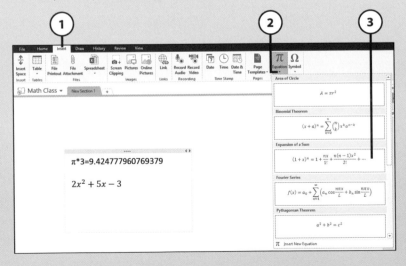

4. OneNote inserts the equation into the note.

5. The Equation Tools open with a Design tab on the Ribbon for further editing and customization.

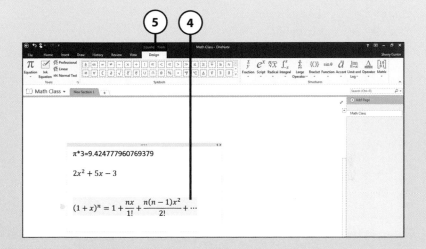

Design Tab

You only see the Equation Tools Design tab if you add an equation using the Equation feature.

Turning Files into Notes

You can import information from other files to use in your OneNote notebooks as notes. When you're compiling notes, such as research for a particular subject or topic, you may need to access files from other programs, such as a paper written in Microsoft Word. OneNote lets you turn a document into pages in your notebook using the File Printout feature. When activated, the file appears to "print" to your OneNote notebook, and each page in the document becomes a page of notes in the current section you're using.

If you would rather not create bunches of pages, you can also choose to embed the file instead. OneNote embeds the file as an icon on the notebook page that, when clicked, opens a program or app to view the file.

Add a File as Notes

You can use the File Printout tool to insert a file as notebook pages. Depending on the file's size, OneNote may create a few or many pages to hold the file's contents.

1. Click or tap Insert.

2. Click or tap File Printout.

3. Navigate to the folder or drive containing the file.

4. Click or tap the file.

5. Click or tap Insert.

6. OneNote "prints" the file as pages in the current section.

Change Your Mind?

If you already added a file's pages as notes, you can easily remove them again. The fastest way to delete the pages is to first select them (click or tap the first page in the Pages pane, hold the Shift key on the keyboard, and then click or tap the last page in the group to be deleted). Once selected, simply press the Delete key on the keyboard. OneNote adds the pages to the Notebook Recycle Bin for permanent deletion later.

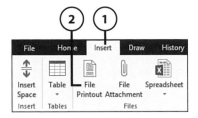

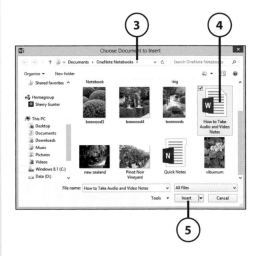

Embed a File

You can embed a file onto a notebook page and use it as a link to the original copy. When you click or tap the embedded file, it opens in the program used to originally create the file.

1. Click or tap Insert.

2. Click or tap File Attachment.

3. Navigate to the folder or drive containing the file.

4. Click or tap the file to embed.

5. Click or tap Insert.

6. The Insert File box appears; click or tap Attach File.

7. The file appears as an icon on the note page; double-click or double-tap the icon to open the file.

What If the Document Changes?

OneNote doesn't maintain a dynamic link to the original file you embed. Any changes made to the original source file are not updated in the embedded file.

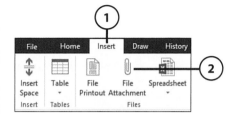

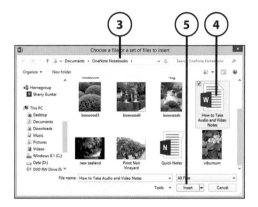

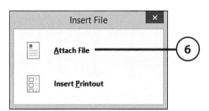

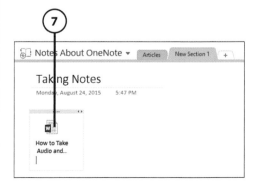

Clipping Web Content with OneNote Clipper

You may not always have the OneNote program open and ready for note taking. You can still add notes to it, though, even if the program window is closed. You can use the OneNote Clipper tool to save web content and store it in a specified notebook. The OneNote Clipper tool is called a *bookmarklet*, a special kind of browser add-on that helps you clip or save web pages and articles.

You can use the OneNote Clipper to save recipes to try later, save an article you want to read when you have time, clip just the story you want to view and not the entire web page, and more. All the items you clip are captured to OneNote and synced across all your devices for easy access. The OneNote Clipper works by capturing an image of the web page and stores a link with the content so you can view the original web page again if needed.

Clip to OneNote button   **OneNote Clipper**

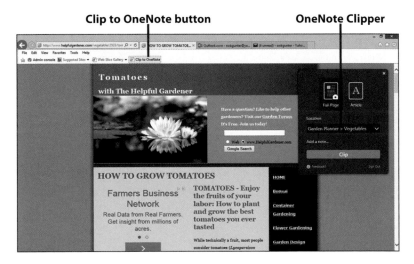

OneNote Clipper is a free tool, but you have to download and install the app to add it to your browser window. You can find the app on the OneNote.com website. Once you add it, a Clip to OneNote button appears on the browser window's Favorites bar. You can use the button to quickly start the OneNote Clipper tool and clip web content into OneNote. Since the OneNote Clipper tool is associated with your Microsoft account, you need to sign in to your account to use the tool.

Add the OneNote Clipper Tool

Downloading and installing the OneNote Clipper tool takes only a few minutes. The Clipper tool works only with the desktop and Microsoft's Internet Explorer browser. When you add the tool, it appears on the browser's Favorites bar.

1. Open your browser window and type www.onenote.com/Clipper/OneNote into the address box.

2. Click or tap the Clip to OneNote link.

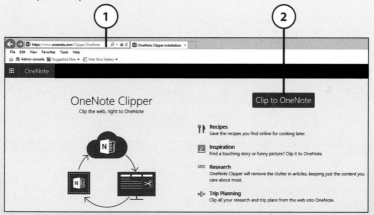

3. Follow the instructions displayed on the web page for installing the app.

4. The OneNote Clipper is added to the Favorites bar as the Clip to OneNote button. If the bar isn't displayed, press Ctrl+Shift+B.

Capture Content with OneNote Clipper

When you find web content you want to capture as a note, you can activate the Clipper tool and specify a notebook and a section for the content. You can also include a brief note about the clipping.

1. Display the web page containing the content you want to clip.

2. Click or tap the Clip to OneNote button on the Favorites bar. If the bar currently isn't displayed, press Ctrl+Shift+B.

3. The first time you use the feature, the Sign In box appears; click or tap Sign In and follow the instructions for signing on to your Microsoft account.

4. To clip the entire web page, click or tap Full Page.

5. To clip just the article, click or tap Article.

6. Click or tap the Location drop-down arrow.

7. Choose a notebook or section.

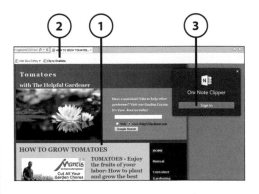

8. Optionally, click Add a Note to add any additional note text.

9. Click or tap Clip.

10. When the clipping is finished, click or tap View in OneNote to open the clipping, or click or tap the Close button to continue web browsing.

Links

When you clip a page or article, OneNote automatically includes a link in the pasted content in your notebook. Just click or tap the link to revisit the original web page.

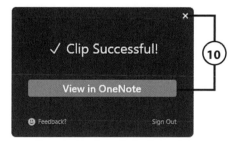

Adding Quick Notes

OneNote has a feature you can use to quickly jot down notes, lists, thoughts, and ideas without needing to place them in a specific notebook, section, or page. Called Quick Notes, they act rather like sticky notes. Offering a much smaller and simplified interface, or mini-window, Quick Notes lets you add text just as you do with a notebook page; click where you want it to go and start typing.

You can post a Quick Note wherever you want on your computer's desktop; it stays open in the background as you work with other windows and programs. You can also pin it in place if you want to keep it visible at all times. When you finish viewing a Quick Note, you can close its window. It's saved with OneNote and kept in the Quick Notes notebook—a special notebook just for unfiled Quick Notes you can access from the Notebooks drop-down list. You can view your Quick Notes later and decide which notebook to put them in or delete them completely.

Quick Note   **Click or tap here to view the Ribbon.**

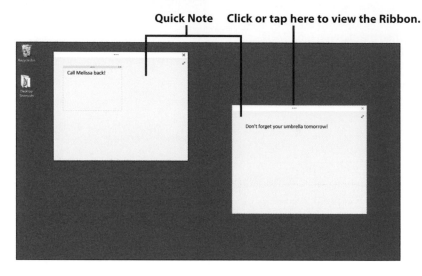

You might use a Quick Note to type in a grocery list and keep it on the desktop while you work, adding to it throughout the day. Or you might jot down a phone number for a colleague you need to call. Perhaps you're brainstorming a new recipe and need to remember your ideas. Quick Notes are a great way to remind yourself about things you want to accomplish without needing to keep a notebook open.

Although a Quick Note mini-window looks rather plain at first, you can quickly summon the Ribbon and apply OneNote tools and features. The Quick Note Ribbon offers a Pages or Navigation pane you can use to navigate through previous Quick Notes and create new ones.

Quick Notes accumulate quickly in the Quick Notes notebook. You can open the notebook any time you want to review notes, clean out old notes, and move or copy important notes to other notebooks.

Add a Quick Note

Use Quick Notes to create instant sticky notes you can leave on the desktop. Quick Notes are automatically saved in the Quick Notes notebook.

1. Click or tap the View tab.

2. Click or tap New Quick Note.

3. Click or tap to start a note and type in your note text.

4. You can leave the Quick Note open for as long as you need it; click or tap Close when you're ready to close the note.

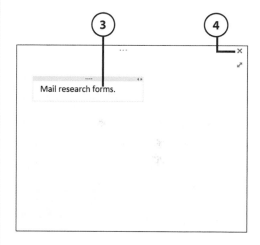

Format a Quick Note

Double-click or double-tap the Quick Note text to display the formatting pop-up toolbar. You can also click or tap the three dots at the top of the Quick Note window to display the Ribbon and click or tap the Home tab to view formatting controls. Use the formatting commands to apply formatting to the note text.

A Quicker Quick Note

If the OneNote program window isn't open, you can still create a Quick Note. Press the Windows key+N to start a new note.

Pin a Quick Note

You can pin a Quick Note in place so it's always in view. The Always on Top command toggles pinning on or off.

1. From the Quick Note window, click or tap the three dots at the top of the window to display the Ribbon.

Different Dots

Be sure to click or tap the three dots at the top of the Quick Note window and not the three dots at the top of the note container box.

2. Click or tap View.

3. Click or tap Always on Top.

4. The Quick Note now stays on top of the display, even if you open other programs and windows. Click or tap Close to close the note when finished using it.

Reposition Notes

You can move Quick Notes around the screen, resize them, and close them when you don't need them. To reposition a note, click and drag its top area, just below the border.

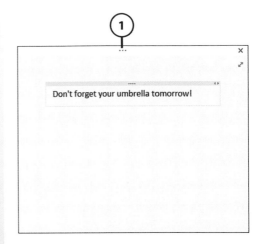

Review Quick Notes

You can review Quick Notes and decide which ones to keep, delete, or move to another notebook. You can view Quick Notes in the Quick Notes Notebook, a special holding area for unfiled Quick Notes that works just a like a regular notebook.

1. With OneNote open, click or tap the Notebooks drop-down arrow.

2. Click or tap Quick Notes.

3. A Quick Notes notebook opens; each Quick Note appears as a page.

4. To remove a note, right-click or press and hold the page tab and choose Delete.

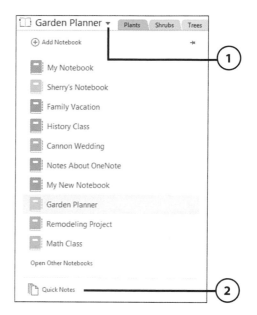

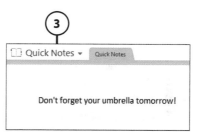

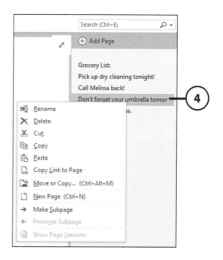

>>>*Go Further*
FILE A QUICK NOTE

You can move a Quick Note to another notebook using the Move or Copy commands. Right-click or press and hold the note's page tab and choose Move or Copy from the shortcut menu. Choose which notebook and section you want the note stored in and click Move.

Turning Notes into Outlook Tasks

If you're also a Microsoft Outlook user, you can turn a OneNote note into an Outlook task. Outlook is Microsoft's personal information manager program and part of the Microsoft Office suite of programs. You can use Outlook to manage email, your calendar, tasks, contacts, and more. If Outlook is already installed on your computer, several additional toolbar buttons appear on OneNote's Home tab. If you're not using Outlook, you won't see the buttons.

Out of all the Microsoft Office programs, OneNote is most tightly integrated with Outlook. That's because the programs utilize a few similar operations and objectives. With the goal of helping you stay organized, both programs include features for creating task lists, for example. You can turn any note text in OneNote into an automatic To-Do list task in Outlook. Using the Outlook Tasks menu button, you can choose the type of task reminder you want to apply, such as Today or Next Week. OneNote adds a flag to mark the text. When you switch over to Outlook, you can see the newly added tasks in the To-Do List.

Turn a Note into an Outlook Task

If you have Outlook installed, you can turn any note text in a notebook into a task that shows up in Outlook's To-Do list.

1. Select the text you want to turn into an Outlook task.

2. Click or tap Home.

3. Click or tap Outlook Tasks.

4. Click or tap a reminder flag.

5. A flag marks the text and OneNote adds the note text as a task in Outlook. You can continue adding more notes as tasks, if needed.

6. Switch over to Outlook to view the task in My Tasks.

Removing Tasks

You can remove a flag from the note text in OneNote without losing the task in Outlook. Simply right-click or press and hold the flag tag and choose Remove Tag. This deletes the flag in OneNote, yet the task remains over in Outlook. If you prefer to remove the task from Outlook but keep the note text in OneNote, right-click or press and hold the flag tag and choose Deleted Outlook Task. This action keeps the note text, but removes the task from Outlook.

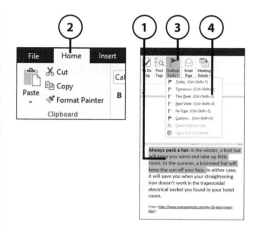

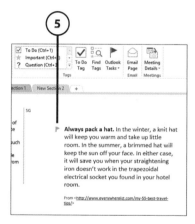

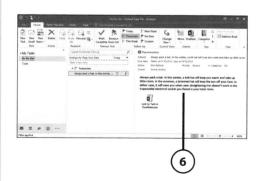

>>>*Go Further*

MORE OUTLOOK OPTIONS

Turning note text into tasks isn't the only feature integrated with Outlook. You can also email a notebook page directly from OneNote using Outlook's messaging capabilities or create meeting notes in OneNote from your Outlook appointments. You can use the Email Page button on the Ribbon's Home tab to create an instant email message using Outlook's Message window. All you have to do is add the recipient's email address and any additional message text. The current notebook page is automatically part of the message. You can use the Message window's tools to apply formatting, attach additional files, or assign priority tags.

If you use Outlook's Calendar to track meetings, you can turn details about the meeting (including date, location, agenda, topic, and attendees) into a OneNote note. Click or tap the Meeting Details button on the Ribbon's Home tab and choose a meeting from the list, or activate the Choose a Meeting from Another Day option.

Look for playback controls on the Ribbon's Playback tab.

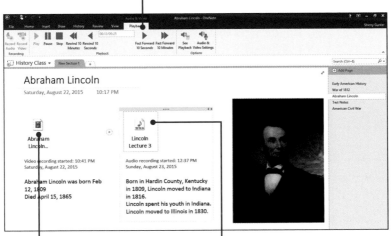

Video clips are displayed with a filmstrip icon.

Audio clips are displayed with a music icon.

In this chapter, you discover how to use OneNote's audio and video recording features. Topics include

→ Recording audio clips
→ Recording video clips
→ Learning how to use playback controls
→ Changing audio and video settings

6

Taking Audio and Video Notes

Not only can you take great notes in OneNote, but you can also record audio and video notes. If you find yourself having to take a class or attend a demonstration, you can quickly turn on OneNote's audio or video features and record the session. Most computers, laptops, tablets, and smartphones have built-in microphones and web cameras, so you don't have to worry about purchasing additional hardware. All you need is your trusty OneNote program running and ready.

OneNote's recording features are perfect for situations like interviews, training demos, brainstorming sessions, or anything you want documentation of to go along with any notes you want to type or write on the page. As you can imagine, audio and video clippings are handy for a wide variety of tasks. In this chapter, you learn how to harness these tools to enhance your own note-taking needs and projects.

Recording Audio and Video Notes

You can record audio and video clips as notes in a notebook. Using your built-in microphone, you can record lectures, meetings, or even dictate your own narration. Audio clips appear on the notebook page with a music note icon so they're easy to identify. The audio clip notes also display the time and date of the recording. You can use the playback controls to listen to audio clips.

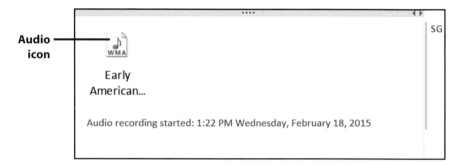

Audio icon

Early American...

Audio recording started: 1:22 PM Wednesday, February 18, 2015

The Record Video feature helps you record video clips using your computer's built-in camera, or the web cam in your tablet or smartphone. Video clips appear on the notebook page identified with a filmstrip icon. Like audio clips, a video recording includes information about when the footage was recorded.

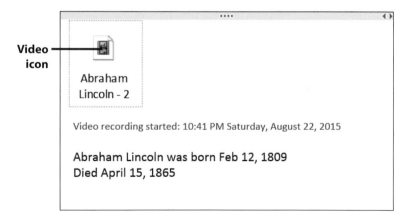

Video icon

Abraham Lincoln - 2

Video recording started: 10:41 PM Saturday, August 22, 2015

**Abraham Lincoln was born Feb 12, 1809
Died April 15, 1865**

When you activate the Record Audio or Record Video commands, OneNote displays a Playback tab on the Ribbon. The Playback tab lists standard playback controls, such as Play, Rewind, and Fast Forward, but instead of a straight-up Rewind or Fast Forward, you have the choice of rewinding/

forwarding 10 seconds or 10 minutes in a clip. You can also view the overall length of the audio or video clip, including the current location in the clip during playback. If you click or tap the clip icon, a pop-up toolbar of playback controls appears and you can quickly click or tap a control. Use this shortcut method if the Playback tab is hidden or you need quick access to the controls.

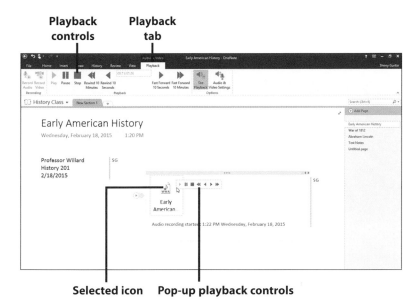

Playback controls   **Playback tab**

Selected icon   Pop-up playback controls

Audio recordings don't take up too much space on your computer or device. A typical 60-minute recording averages about 5MB. Video clips, surprisingly, don't take up a lot of disk space either; a 60-minute video recording consumes about 60MB. If you adjust the quality settings, the recording can take up a greater amount of disk space. Broadcast quality video, for example, quickly eats up disk space.

The clips you record, whether they're a few seconds in length or hours long, are given default names. The names are based on the notebook page on which they are added. For example, if you record an audio clip on a page named History Class, the audio clip is automatically named History Class. You can replace the default name with a unique name to help you identify the clip's contents. You can also edit the default information written below the audio or video clip icon.

As you're recording, you can take notes to coincide with the task at hand. You can write or type notes and the notes are linked to the recording. This behind-the-scenes feature lets you use notes like a table of contents, letting you jump to a spot in the recording where the note was recorded along with it. You can add your text notes directly in the box containing the audio or video clip, or you can add your notes in separate note boxes. In either scenario, any additional notes taken during the recording session are linked to the clip. A playback icon appears next to linked notes when you hover the mouse pointer over the note. You can use the playback icon to play the recording at that particular point corresponding to when the note was taken.

Clip name   Recording information   Notes linked to the recording

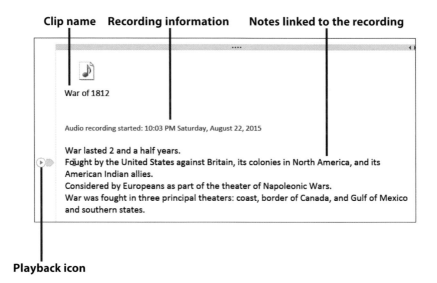

War of 1812

Audio recording started: 10:03 PM Saturday, August 22, 2015

War lasted 2 and a half years.
Fought by the United States against Britain, its colonies in North America, and its American Indian allies.
Considered by Europeans as part of the theater of Napoleonic Wars.
War was fought in three principal theaters: coast, border of Canada, and Gulf of Mexico and southern states.

Playback icon

Record Audio

You can use the Ribbon's Insert tab to start an audio recording. Audio clips, just like other notes you take in OneNote, appear in their own container box, which can be moved, resized, or renamed on a page.

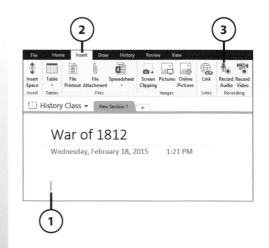

1. Click or tap the area on the note page where you want the audio icon to appear.

2. Click or tap Insert.

3. Click or tap Record Audio.

4. OneNote starts recording and displays the Audio & Video commands on the Ribbon.

5. As you're recording audio, you can take additional notes directly in the audio note box or elsewhere on the page as needed, and the notes are automatically synced with the portion of the recording in which you took them. (Learn about playing linked notes later in this chapter.)

6. When you finish recording, click or tap Stop.

7. The audio clip automatically uses the page name as part of its default filename.

Recording Tips

You may need to make a few adjustments to get the best recordings. For example, whether you're doing a one-on-one interview or recording a classroom lecture, make sure the built-in microphone is at the right distance from the speaker. This might include moving closer to the podium.

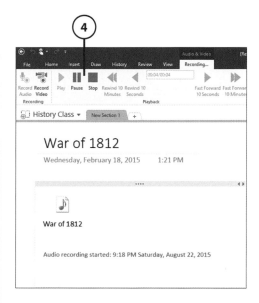

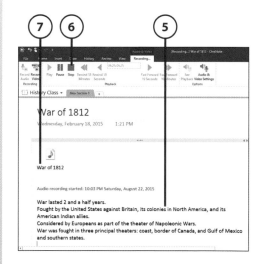

Record Video

Recording video is nearly identical to recording audio clips; however, you use your built-in camera as well as your built-in microphone to record. Depending on the camera's placement, you may need to reposition your device to face the right direction to record video footage.

1. Click or tap the area on the note page where you want the video icon added.

2. Click or tap Insert.

3. Click or tap Record Video.

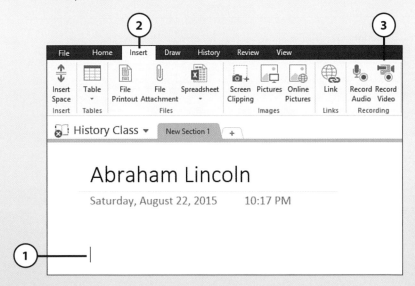

4. OneNote opens a video window and starts recording.

5. The Audio & Video Recording commands appear on the Ribbon.

6. In addition to recording video, you can also take notes directly in the video note box, or elsewhere on the page as needed.

7. When you finish recording, click or tap Stop.

Video Window Positioning

You can move the video window out of the way when recording notes, if needed. For example, you can minimize the window or snap it to the side of the screen while taking notes on the other side of the screen. Even though it's minimized, the feature is still recording.

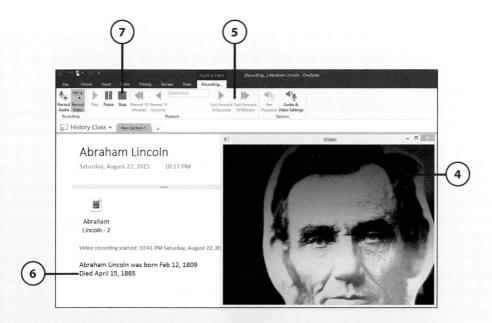

8. The video clip automatically uses the page name as part of its default filename.

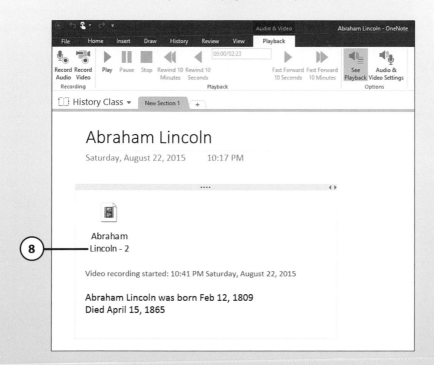

It's Not All Good

Video Recording Cautions

Unlike the audio recording, you cannot pause the video recording feature. Do not close the video window or the recording will stop immediately. Also, if you click or tap the Start menu, the video recording stops.

Working with Audio and Video Clips

After you record an audio or video clip, you can play the recording using OneNote's playback controls. Whenever you insert an audio or video clip, the Playback tab is automatically added to the Ribbon. You won't see the tab on a page without an audio or video clip.

Whenever you want to view details about the recording, you can hover the mouse pointer over the audio or video icon. A pop-up box displays the clip's name, when it was created, and its size. You can also display a pop-up toolbar of playback controls when you click or tap the audio or video clip icon.

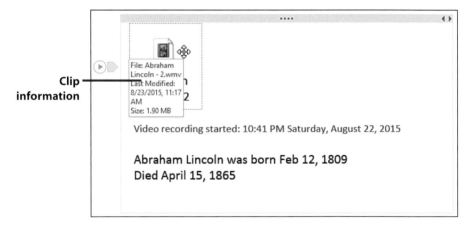

Remember, audio and video clips can be treated just like any other note. They can be moved around on a page, copied and pasted to other pages, resized, and deleted.

Use Playback Controls

You can use OneNote's playback controls to listen or view audio and video clips, respectively. Playback controls feature the typical command buttons you expect to find on any recording device. For example, the Play button starts the playback, while the Pause button pauses the playback.

1. Click or tap the clip you want to play.

2. Click or tap the Playback tab on the Ribbon.

3. Click or tap Play.

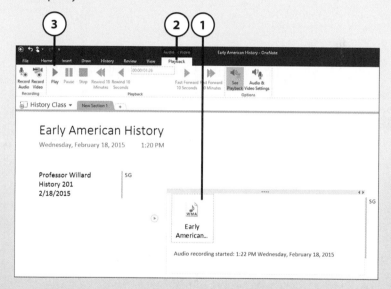

4. To pause the playback, click or tap Pause; to resume play again, click or tap the Pause button a second time.

5. To rewind the clip, click or tap Rewind 10 Seconds.

6. To forward the clip, click or tap Fast Forward 10 Seconds.

7. To stop the clip, click or tap Stop.

8. View the clip duration and current location here.

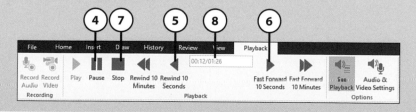

Pin the Playback Controls

You can always pin the Ribbon onscreen for as long as you need to access the playback controls. Click or tap the Pin the Ribbon icon at the far right side of the Ribbon, or press Ctrl+F1 on the keyboard.

Play Linked Notes

If you added notes during a recording session, you can listen to or view specific parts of the audio or video clip that coincide with a text note. Linked notes offer their own playback control that lets you jump to a specific part of the recording.

1. Move the mouse pointer over the linked note until a Play button appears, or click or tap in the linked note text.

2. Click or tap Play.

3. OneNote highlights the note and starts the clip at the point the note was taken.

4. To stop the clip at any time, click or tap Stop.

See Playback

Turn on the See Playback command to have your linked notes highlighted during playback. Click or tap the See Playback button on the Ribbon's Playback tab. OneNote highlights each note taken during the recording session that corresponds with the playback. This works only with notes that link with the recording.

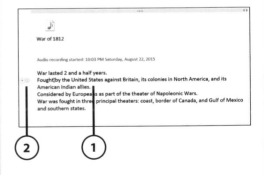

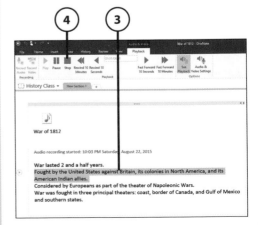

Rename a Clip

You can change the default name of an audio or video clip to something more recognizable using the Rename command. For example, if you're recording a product demonstration, you might name the clip Demo1 or use the product name. In the case of a lecture, you might assign the class name or the professor's name as the clip title.

1. Right-click or press and hold the clip icon.

2. Click or tap Rename from the shortcut menu.

3. Type in a unique name for the clip.

4. Click or tap OK.

5. The clip is renamed and the audio or video icon displays the newly assigned title.

Editing Default Clip Text

Just below every audio or video clip note icon is a default line of text detailing when the clip was recorded. You can edit this text to say something else. For example, you might want to replace it with a description of the clip's contents. To edit the text, select it and type in the new text to replace it.

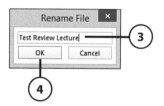

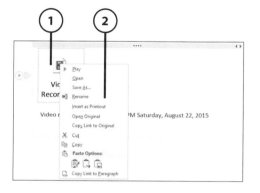

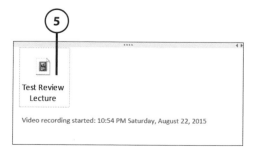

Delete a Clip

You can remove video or audio clips you no longer want to keep as notes. Any deletions you make are permanently removed.

1. Right-click or press and hold the clip's note box border.

2. Click or tap Delete from the shortcut menu.

3. OneNote removes the clip and the cursor marks its former spot.

More Shortcuts

You can also click or tap the audio or video note and press the Delete key on the keyboard to remove the clip. If you accidentally remove a clip, quickly press Ctrl+Z to undo the action.

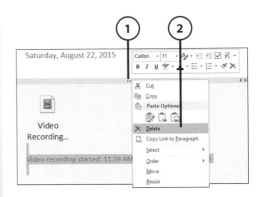

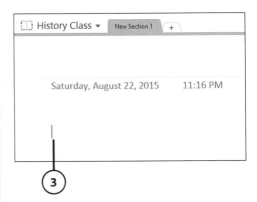

CUT, COPY, AND PASTE

You can cut, copy, and paste clips. You can paste them onto other note pages or into other notebooks. Click or tap the clip and press Ctrl+X to cut the clip, or press Ctrl+C to copy it. Next, click where you want the clip to go and press Ctrl+V.

Open a Clip in Another App

Although you may have recorded a clip in OneNote, you can also use another app to open and play the clip. For example, you may want to open a clip in the Windows Media Player or another program for playing a clip.

1. Right-click or press and hold the clip icon.

2. Click or tap Open from the shortcut menu.

3. A warning prompt box appears; click OK to continue.

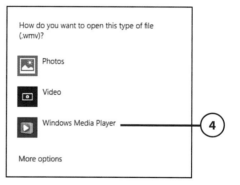

4. Click or tap the app you want to use to play the clip. (If you already have a designated default app for playback, it might open automatically and play the clip.)

5. The app opens and plays the clip. In this example, Windows Media Player opens.

Adding Previously Recorded Clips

You can always add previously recorded clips from other sources and place them on your pages using the Copy and Paste commands. You can also link to clips found elsewhere on the Web. Learn more about linking in Chapter 9, "Working with Links."

Embed a Clip

You can embed an audio or video clip from another source and add it to your note page. Using the File Attachment tool, you can embed an audio or video file stored on your computer or another device, such as a USB drive.

1. Click or tap where you want to embed the file.

2. Click or tap Insert.

3. Click or tap File Attachment.

4. Navigate to the folder or drive containing the file you want to use.

5. Click or tap the file.

6. Click or tap Insert.

7. The Insert File dialog box appears; click or tap Attach File.

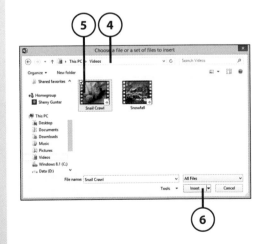

8. The file appears embedded on the page. Double-click or double-tap the embedded clip to view or listen to the clip.

9. A warning prompt box might appear; click OK to continue.

10. Click or tap the app you want to use to play the clip. (If you already have a designated default app for playback, it might open automatically and play the clip.)

11. The app opens and plays the clip. In this example, Windows Video opens. Click or tap Close when finished.

No Playback

Embedded audio or video clips do not activate the Playback tab on the Ribbon. Instead, you must activate the embedded file to play it.

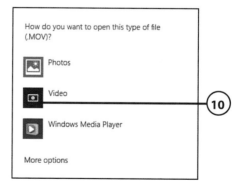

Find Audio and Video Settings

If you ever need to fine-tune your audio or video settings, you can open the Audio and Video settings in the OneNote Options dialog box. Use the settings in this dialog box to change recording devices, such as switching to another microphone, or change the recording format.

1. Click or tap the Playback tab.

2. Click or tap Audio & Video Settings.

3. The OneNote Options dialog box opens to the Audio & Video category.

4. Click or tap the setting you want to edit and make your changes.

5. Click OK to exit the dialog box and apply your changes.

Another Route

Another way to get to the Audio & Video settings is by clicking or tapping the File tab and then clicking or tapping the Options tab.

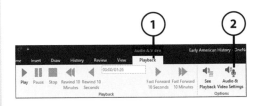

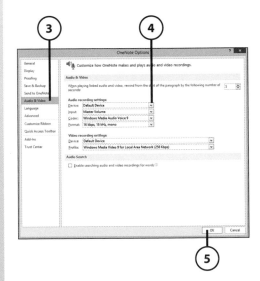

>>>*Go Further*

SEARCHING AUDIO AND VIDEO CLIPS

You can search through your recordings for spoken words that meet designated search criteria. For example, you might search through your recordings of a lecture series to find information for an assignment or test. When you enable the Audio Search tool, you can conduct a search through each clip on a page as well as any page notes.

By default, the feature is not turned on because it has to work a bit harder to find search terms among audio recordings. A particularly long lecture, for example, may take awhile to search through depending on the audio quality. You can enable Audio Search using the Audio & Video settings in the OneNote Options dialog box. Simply check the Enable Searching Audio and Video Recordings for Words Check box. To learn more about searching notes, see Chapter 10, "Tagging and Searching Notes."

Freeform drawing

Drawing tools

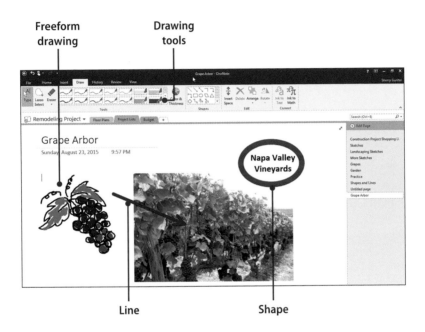

Line

Shape

In this chapter, you learn how to put OneNote's many drawing tools to use. Topics include

→ Doodling and sketching with freeform drawings

→ Drawing shapes and lines

→ Selecting drawings, shapes, and lines

→ Erasing parts of your drawings with the Eraser tool

→ Resizing and moving drawings

→ Rearranging drawn items in layers

Drawing Notes

You're not just limited to notes composed of text, pictures, or audio and video clips. You can also draw your own notes. OneNote offers several tools you can use to create your own drawings on your notebook pages. You can create freeform sketches, draw shapes and lines, and combine or arrange them to create layered drawings, and more. Whether you're using a mouse, a stylus, or just your finger on a touchscreen device, OneNote makes it easy to create illustrated notes of your own design.

Drawing Freeform Notes

Back in Chapter 4, "Taking Notes," you learned how to take handwritten notes using the Pen tool. You can use this same tool to draw sketches, doodles, and other freeform drawings on your notebook pages. You can draw freeform lines on top of existing notes, or by themselves on an empty area of your notebook page.

Freeform drawings are composed entirely of lines. Unlike shapes or straight lines you can draw with other tools, freeform lines can go all over the place, hence the name "freeform." You can control the line thickness of the Pen tool, as well as choose an ink color.

Pen tools　　　　　　　　　**Freeform drawing**

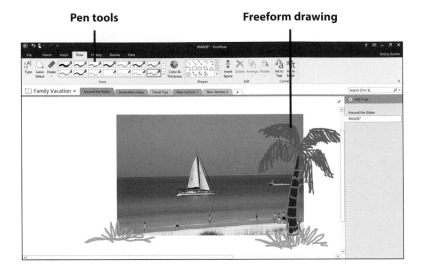

Freeform drawing isn't always easy for most people, unless you're an artistic type to start with; however, don't let that stop you from utilizing OneNote's drawing tools. Depending on how you like to draw and the type of device you're using, you have several options to try. If you're using a touchscreen computer, laptop, tablet, or smartphone, you may prefer using a stylus to create freeform drawings. Acting much like a real pen, the stylus draws directly on the screen, giving you greater control of the lines you draw and the amount of detail you can create.

If a stylus isn't available, you can use your finger to draw on a touchscreen. As with finger paintings, drawings you create with the touch of your finger may be less detailed than those you create with a stylus.

If you aren't using a touchscreen device, you can use the mouse to draw. This takes a little more practice, but you can draw all kinds of freehand sketches, lines, and doodles with just the mouse.

Different line thicknesses can create differences in the smoothness and details of your sketches and doodles. A thicker line may result in a smoother-looking drawing, while a thinner line may show the shakiness of your drawing hand. You may need to experiment with the different settings to see which freeform line thickness works best for you.

0.7 mm line   **1.0 mm line**   **1.5 mm line**

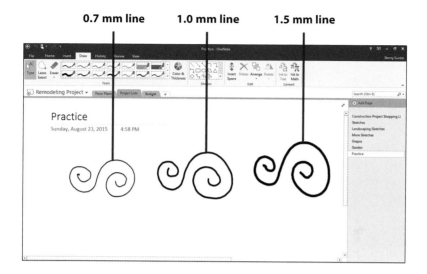

After you create a freeform drawing, you can select the entire drawing or portions of the drawing to move, resize, or make changes to the lines.

Draw a Freeform Note

You can draw a freeform note in the form of a sketch, doodle, scribble, or any other type of drawing.

1. Click or tap the Ribbon's Draw tab.

2. Click or tap a Pen to use from the Gallery.

3. To view a greater pen selection, click or tap the More button.

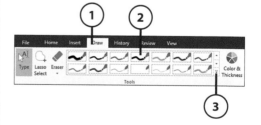

4. The full gallery of pen styles appears; click or tap a pen from the list.

5. The mouse pointer takes the shape of a pen tip; to draw, click or tap where you want to start and begin drawing.

6. When you complete the drawing, you can click or tap the Drawing tab's Type command to return to typing mode.

Drawing Tip

For some users, choosing a thicker pen style may work better for creating smooth lines in the drawing. A thinner line may more readily show an unsteady hand. You might also be able to adjust the sensitivity of your touchscreen or stylus to help with drawing tasks. Check your device's documentation to learn more about finding these settings.

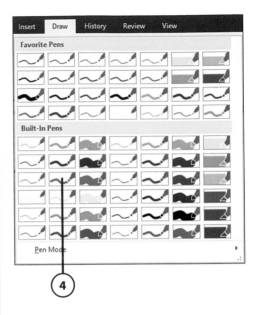

Change the Pen Color and Thickness

You can change the Pen tool's color and thickness using the Color & Thickness dialog box.

1. Click or tap Draw.

2. Click or tap Color & Thickness.

3. With the Pen option selected, click or tap the thickness you want to use.

4. Click or tap a color from the palette.

5. Click or tap OK.

6. You can now draw with the new settings applied.

Highlighters

Some of the Pen tool styles are highlighters, designed to help you highlight text in a note. Highlighters appear thick in line weight. You might find the highlighter styles useful for other types of drawings, or for creating stylized scripts when handwriting notes.

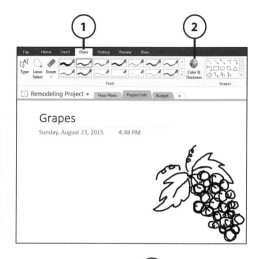

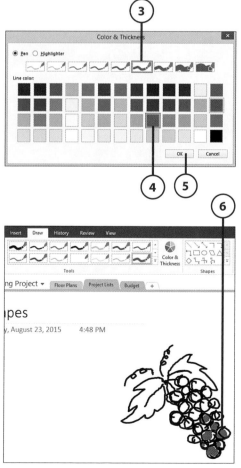

Drawing Shapes and Lines

OneNote offers a library of preset shapes and lines you can draw on your notebook pages. Shapes include basics like the oval, rectangle, and triangle, and variations of arrows pointing in different directions. The library even includes a few chart-building shapes for graphing purposes. You can combine several shapes to create different types of drawings in OneNote. For example, you can position one shape on top of another to create an entirely different shape.

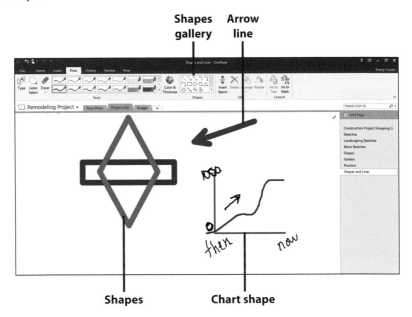

All the tools for drawing shapes and lines are located on the Ribbon's Draw tab. When you draw a shape, the shape tool you choose is active only for the one drawing. You cannot keep drawing more of the same shape without selecting the tool again.

You can choose a line thickness for the shape or line you draw before actually drawing the shape on the page. Shapes and lines are drawn with the same Pen tool, so you can specify a color or thickness from either the gallery list box or the Color & Thickness dialog box. You can also apply the settings to a line or shape already appearing on the notebook page.

Draw a Shape

Use the Shapes gallery to choose a shape to draw. Although the gallery is not as populated with shapes as the other Microsoft Office programs, it still features several basics that you can easily put to use. When you finish drawing a shape, it's automatically selected for you in case you want to perform more edits on the drawing.

1. Click or tap Draw.

2. Click or tap the More button in the Shapes gallery list.

3. Click or tap a shape.

4. The mouse pointer takes the shape of a crosshair icon; click or tap where you want the drawing to start.

5. Drag the shape until you create the size and shape you want to use.

No Fill Color

With other Office programs, like Word or Excel, you can add a fill color to the shape's interior area. OneNote does not feature this tool; however, you can color in the interior using the Pen tool.

Pen Properties

You can right-click or press and hold a selected shape or line to reveal a pop-up toolbar that includes access to the Pen tool's line thickness and color. Click or tap the Pen Properties command to change the selected item's formatting.

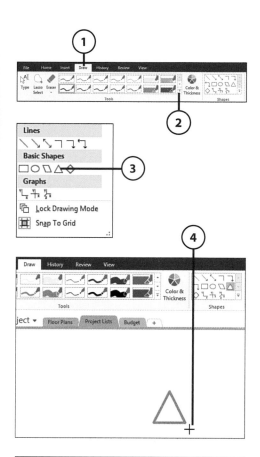

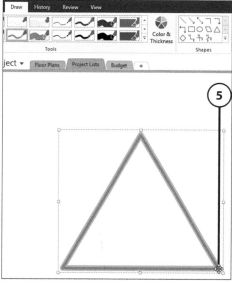

Draw a Line

Lines are the simplest way to draw on a page. You can choose from arrows, bent lines, or plain, straight lines. You might use an arrow, for example, to point to another note or an important part of an article or picture. When you finish drawing a line, it's automatically selected for you in case you want to perform more edits on the drawing.

1. Click or tap Draw.

2. Click or tap a line style from the Shapes gallery list.

3. The mouse pointer takes the shape of a crosshairs icon; click or tap where you want the drawing to start.

4. Drag the shape until you create the size and shape you want to use.

5. Release the mouse button or your finger from the touchscreen and OneNote creates the shape.

Rotate It

You can rotate lines you draw in OneNote by dragging either end of the line. Depending on the direction you drag, you can rotate the line in varying degrees.

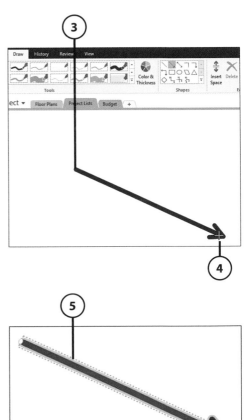

Working with Drawings

You can apply a variety of features and commands to enhance the drawings, shapes, and lines you add to a notebook page. For example, you can rotate a shape or arrange two or more shapes on top of each other to create a drawing. You can also move and resize your drawings.

Many of the tasks you need to perform with lines and shapes require you to group them. Depending on the complexity of your drawing, you can group your lines and drawings with a box, a freeform selection lasso, or you can simply select a single line or shape in which to edit.

Select Lines and Shapes with a Selection Box

To apply any sort of commands or features to more than one line or shape in your drawing, you need to select all the lines to be included in the action. If you want to move a drawing, for example, you need to select all its parts before attempting to move it. OneNote lets you group things you want to keep together in a selection box. The shapes and lines are not permanently grouped, but grouped just for the task at hand.

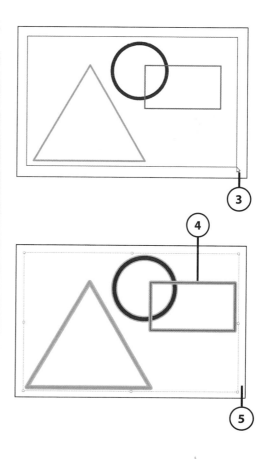

1. Click or tap Draw.

2. Click or tap Type.

3. Click and drag a box around all the items you want to group.

4. OneNote selects all the items within the box area.

5. Click or tap anywhere outside the box to deselect the items again.

Select Lines and Shapes with a Lasso

Another tool you can use to select a group of lines and shapes is the Lasso Select tool located on the Draw tab. Instead of a box, this tool draws a freeform border around the items you want to select. This is handy for lines and shapes that don't fit well into a selection box, or interact too closely with other notes or nearby shapes.

1. Click or tap Draw.

2. Click or tap Lasso Select.

3. Click and drag the lasso around all the items you want to group.

4. Click or tap to complete the loop.

5. All the items within the loop are selected and surrounded with a selection box.

6. Click or tap the Lasso Select button again to turn off the feature.

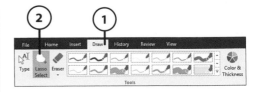

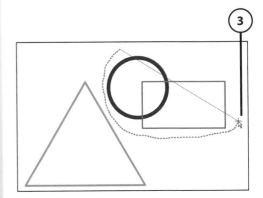

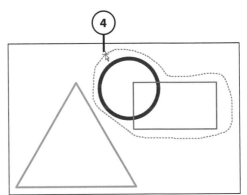

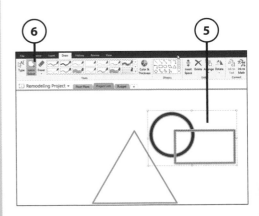

Select Individual Lines and Shapes

You can select a single line or shape to apply a command or feature, such as changing a line's color or rotating a shape. Unlike the grouping technique, selecting a single line or shape is just a click or tap away.

1. Click or tap Draw.

2. Click or tap Type.

3. Click or tap the line or shape you want to select.

4. The line or shape is immediately selected.

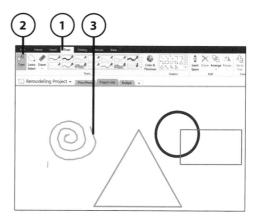

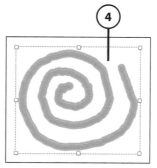

Use the Eraser Tool

The Eraser tool lets you edit or remove unwanted parts of your drawings. You might erase a line between two drawn shapes to create a larger shape, for instance. Or you might erase a portion of a sketch or doodle to draw it over again. You can erase a small portion or the entire drawing; don't worry about moving the eraser over other types of notes. Only drawings are erased with the tool.

1. Click or tap Draw.

2. Click or tap the Eraser drop-down arrow.

3. Click or tap an eraser size.

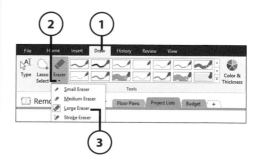

4. The mouse pointer takes the shape of square eraser; click and drag over the area of the drawing you want to erase.

5. OneNote removes the line or lines you drag over.

6. Continue erasing as much as you need to remove from the drawing.

7. Click or tap the Eraser button to toggle the feature off again.

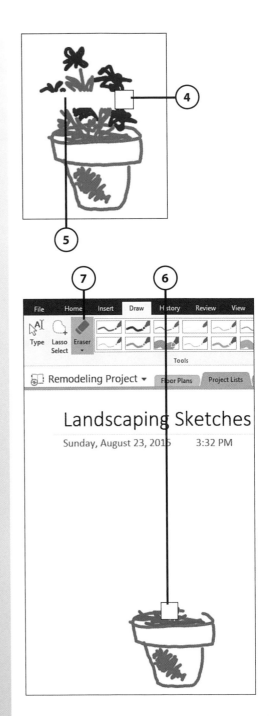

It's Not All Good

Oops!

If you accidentally erase an important part of your drawing, click or tap the Undo button on the Quick Access toolbar or press Ctrl+Z on the keyboard. OneNote immediately undoes the last action for you.

Delete Drawings

To completely remove a drawing, you can apply the Delete command.

1. Select the drawing, line, or shape you want to delete.

2. Click or tap Draw.

3. Click or tap Delete.

4. OneNote removes the drawing.

Delete Key Shortcut

You can also press the Delete key on the keyboard to instantly remove the selected drawing, line, or shape.

Pop-Up Shortcut

You can right-click or press and hold a selected shape or line to reveal a pop-up toolbar that includes the Delete command. Click or tap Delete from the toolbar to remove the selected item.

Move Drawings

You can move drawings, lines, and shapes and place them elsewhere on a page, on other notes, or on other drawings.

1. Select the drawing, line, or shape you want to move.

2. Move the mouse pointer over the selected item until the mouse pointer becomes a four-sided arrow icon.

3. Drag the drawing to a new location on the page.

4. Drop the drawing in place and it's instantly moved; click anywhere outside the selection box to deselect the drawing.

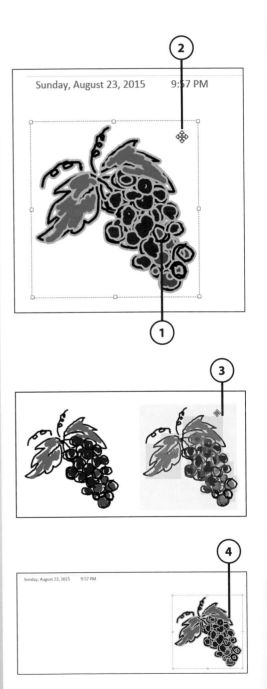

>>>Go Further
COPY INSTEAD

To make a copy of the selected drawing, right-click or press and hold the drawing to display a shortcut menu. Click or tap Copy from the menu. Next, click or tap where you want the copy to go and follow the same technique, this time using the Paste command to paste the drawing.

Resize Your Drawings

You can make your drawings, lines, and shapes bigger or smaller by resizing them. You can use any of the selection handles surrounding a selected drawing to resize; use the corner handles to resize bigger or smaller, or use the side selection handles to resize up and down or right and left.

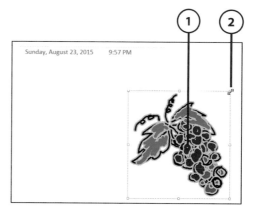

1. Select the drawing, line, or shape you want to resize.

2. Move the mouse pointer over a selection box handle until it takes the shape of a double-sided arrow icon.

3. Drag the selection handle to resize the drawing.

4. When you finish dragging, the drawing is resized; click anywhere outside the selection box to deselect the drawing.

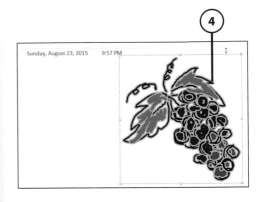

Rotate Drawings

You can rotate a line, shape, or drawing or flip its direction horizontally or vertically on the page.

1. Select the drawing, line, or shape you want to rotate.

2. Click or tap Draw.

3. Click or tap the Rotate drop-down arrow.

4. Click or tap a rotation setting.

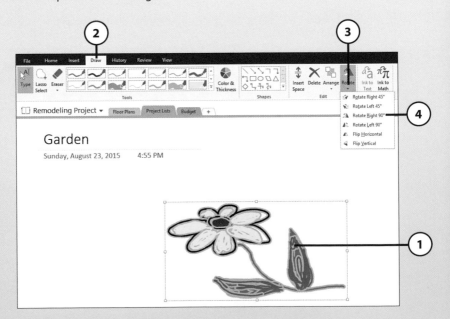

5. OneNote rotates the selected item; click anywhere outside the selection box to deselect the drawing.

Layer Lines and Shapes

If you position a shape on top of another shape, you can adjust the layering to determine which shape appears at the top of the stack and which appears at the back of the stack. Use the Arrange command to move shapes, lines, or drawings forward or backward.

1. Select the drawing, line, or shape you want to arrange.

2. Click or tap Draw.

3. Click or tap the Arrange drop-down arrow.

4. Click or tap a position.

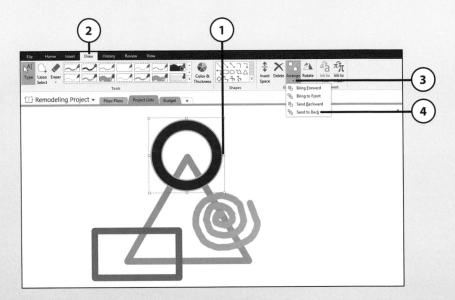

5. OneNote moves the selected item forward or backward in the arrangement; click anywhere outside the selection box to deselect the drawing.

Stacking Tips

You can move drawings to the front, middle, or back of a stack, depending on how many items you're arranging. You can also arrange more than just lines and shapes. You can stack drawings on top or behind other types of notes on a page.

Table   Spreadsheet

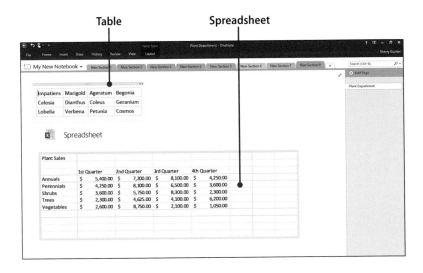

This chapter shows you how to include tabular and numeric data in your notebooks in the form of tables and spreadsheets. Topics include

→ Using tables

→ Adding rows and columns

→ Formatting tables

→ Inserting Excel spreadsheets

→ Importing spreadsheets

→ Editing spreadsheets

→ Creating charts

Working with Tables and Spreadsheets

Freeform notes are fine for some types of information, but other notes are better expressed in a more structured format. Some data is easier to read in tabular format; other data requires the formal calculation power of a spreadsheet.

For these types of notes, OneNote lets you create both simple tables and more complex Excel spreadsheets. Create a table and enter your notes into the organized rows and columns. Or create or import an Excel spreadsheet for number-heavy notes.

Using Tables

When you need to organize your notes in rows and columns, create a table in OneNote and then fill up the individual cells. Tables provide a more rigid structure for notes that benefit from uniform spacing and layout. Tables are great vehicles for the presentation of information; they create graphic interest (especially when the borders are turned on) and are the perfect tool for bringing order and organization to ungainly note lists. For example, you might use a table to present a list of note items, such a list of popular annual flowers or a side-by-side list of products. Tables in their simplest form are a grid of intersecting rows and columns. The areas made by this interconnectivity are called *cells*. You can fill table cells with text, numbers, pictures, and so on.

The Table Tool's Layout tab offers numerous table tools

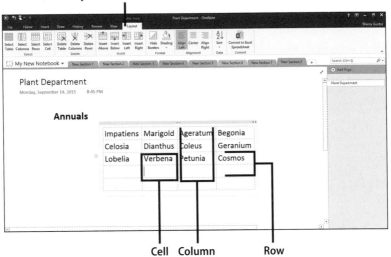

Despite the rigidity of a table's overall structure—a rectangle or square in shape—individual columns and rows are easy to resize to fit whatever note text, picture, or link you're inserting into individual cells. It's also easy to add more columns and rows as you need them or remove columns and rows you don't want in the table. You can choose to create tables with or without borders, add background shading, and assign other formatting to make the presentation look good. When you add a table to a notebook page, a Layout tab of Table Tools appears on the Ribbon, offering tools to help you. In this section, you'll learn all about ways to build and edit tables.

Create a Table

Creating a table is as easy as "drawing" it in your notes. Just specify how many rows and columns you need.

1. In an open notebook, click or tap where you want to insert the table.

2. Click or tap the Insert tab.

3. Click or tap the Table drop-down arrow.

4. Drag the mouse over the boxes to select how many rows and columns you want in the new table.

5. The new table is immediately inserted into your notebook and ready for you to add notes to the cells.

6. You can use the Layout tab to apply commands and features to your table.

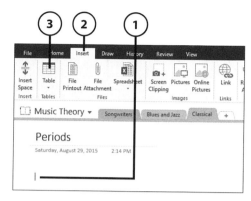

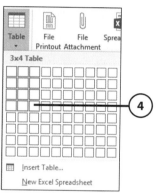

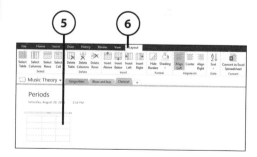

Enter Data into a Table

Once you've inserted a table into a notebook, you can enter any kinds of notes into the individual cells. You can enter words, numbers, even pictures. The cells of the table resize automatically to fit the notes you enter.

1. Click or tap within the cell in the table in which you want to enter data and type your note text.

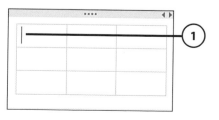

2. Press Tab to move to the next cell in the table and continue adding text or other notes.

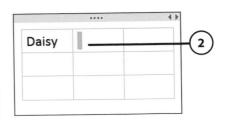

Images in Tables

Table cells can hold any type of note normally placed on a notebook page. For example, a table can hold any type of link or image, such as a picture stored on your computer or cloud storage account, a picture from the Web, or even a screen clipping. Use the appropriate options on the Ribbon's Insert tab to insert pictures, links, and the like.

Select Rows and Columns

There are several operations you may want to perform on entire rows and columns. For example, you may want to select a row to change cell text alignment or bold the text in a given column. OneNote offers several ways to select entire rows and columns. In this example, you learn how to use the Layout tab's Select tools to select rows and columns.

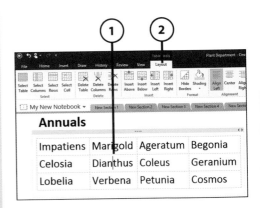

1. Click or tap a cell in the column or row you want to select.

2. Click or tap the Layout tab.

3. To select a column, click or tap Select Columns.

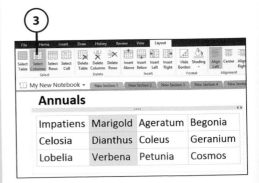

4. To select a row, click or tap Select Rows.

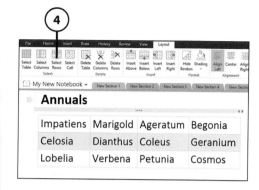

More Selection Options

You can also use the mouse pointer to select columns and rows in a table. To select a column, move the mouse pointer above the column you want to select until the pointer becomes a downward-pointing arrow icon and click or tap to select the column. To select a row, move the mouse pointer to the far left of the row until the pointer looks like a large right-pointing triangle; click or tap to select the row.

Selecting Table Text

You can select text within table cells just like you do with any other note text. To quickly select a single word, for example, double-click or double-tap the word. You can also select an entire cell; click or tap in a cell and then click or tap the Select Cell button on the Layout tab.

Formatting Row and Column Contents

When you select an entire column or row, you can apply text formatting to all the contents of that selection. If you want to bold all the text in a header row, for example, select the row and then press Ctrl+B; all the text in that row is now bold.

Selecting Table Elements

You can use a variety of methods to select table text, but the Layout tab offers four command buttons for selecting rows, columns, cells or the entire table. Simply click or tap the command you want to apply.

Change Text Alignment

By default, the text in a table's cells is left aligned. You can, however, change the alignment for any selected cell or group of cells to be either centered or right aligned.

1. Select the table cells you want to realign.

2. Click or tap the Layout tab.

3. Click or tap an alignment option; click Align Left, Center, or Align Right.

4. The alignment is immediately applied to the selected cell or cells. You can click anywhere outside of selection to unselect the cells.

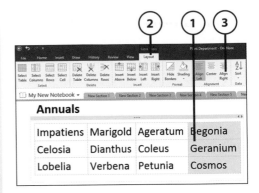

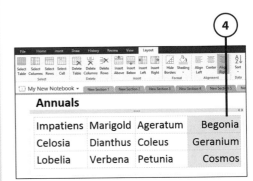

Sort Table Data

Once you've entered data in a table, you may want to sort that data in a specific order. OneNote lets you sort by any column in ascending or descending order.

1. Click or tap any cell within the column by which you want to sort.

2. Click or tap the Layout tab.

3. Click or tap Sort.

4. Click or tap Sort Ascending to sort from smallest to largest, or in A to Z alphabetical order.

5. Click or tap Sort Descending to sort from largest to smallest, or in Z to A reverse alphabetical order.

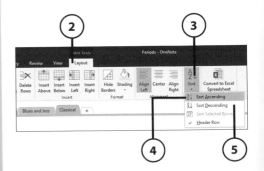

Insert a Row

When you first insert a table, you determine how many rows (and columns) will be in that table. Later, if you need more rows to hold your tabular notes, you can insert new rows into your existing table.

1. Select a row adjacent to where you want to insert the new row.

2. Click or tap the Layout tab.

3. Click or tap Insert Above to insert a new row above the selected row.

4. Click or tap Insert Below to insert a new row below the selected row.

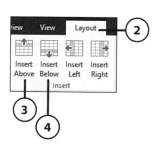

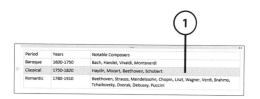

Append Extra Rows

To add a new row at the bottom of a table, click or tap in the last cell in the last row of the table and then press Tab. This creates a new row beneath that row and moves the cursor to the first cell in that new row.

Insert a Column

Just as you can insert new rows into a table, you can also insert new columns.

1. Select a column adjacent to where you want to insert the new column.

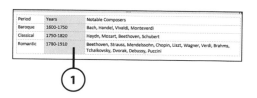

2. Click or tap the Layout tab.

3. Click or tap Insert Left to insert a column to the left of the selected column.

4. Click or tap Insert Right to insert a column to the right of the selected column.

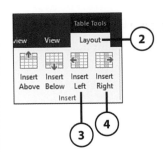

Table Shortcuts

If you select a column or row and right-click (or press and hold if you're using a touchscreen), the shortcut menu appears. Click or tap the Table command to view a menu list of common table actions, such as Insert Left or Insert Right.

Delete Rows and Columns

If you find that you have more rows or columns than you need in a table, you can delete unwanted ones. Any notes in that row or column are also deleted, of course.

1. Select the row or column you want to delete.

2. Click or tap the Layout tab.

3. Click or tap Delete Columns to remove the selected column.

4. Click or tap Delete Rows to remove the selected row.

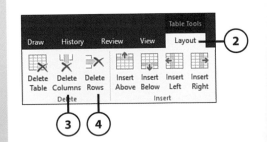

Hide Table Borders

By default, any table you insert has a thin border around each cell (and around the entire table, too). If you prefer to view the table's contents without these borders, you can opt to hide the borders.

1. Select the table or click or tap any cell within the table.

2. Click or tap the Layout tab.

3. Click or tap Hide Borders.

4. OneNote hides the table borders; click or tap the button again to display the borders.

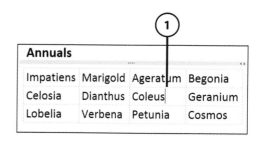

Add Cell Shading

To highlight important information in a table, format specific cells with different color shading. Cell shading applies to the background behind the cell's contents.

1. Select the cell or cells you want to format.

2. Click or tap the Layout tab.

3. Click or tap the Shading drop-down arrow to display the Theme Colors palette.

4. If the color you want to use is shown in the palette, click or tap to select the shading color and it's immediately applied to the selected cells.

5. If the color you want is not shown on the palette, click or tap More Colors to open the Colors dialog box.

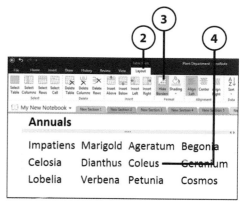

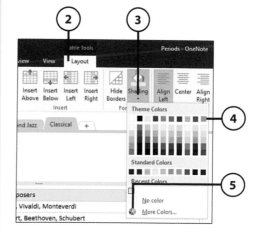

6. Click or tap the Standard tab to select a color from the standard color palette; click or tap a color from the palette.

7. Click or tap the Custom tab to select a custom color from the custom colors palette; click or tap the color you want to apply.

8. Click OK to exit the dialog box and apply the shading color.

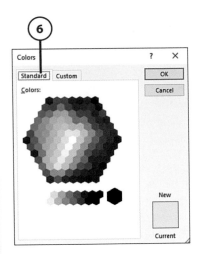

Removing Shading

You can remove a shading color and return the selected cell(s) to the default status (no color). Display the Shading drop-down menu and click or tap No color.

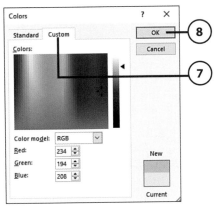

Convert a Table to a Spreadsheet

If you enter numeric data into a table, you may later find that you want to use those numbers in calculations of various sorts. Unfortunately, you cannot perform calculations on numbers in a table.

To perform numeric calculations on table data, you need to convert the table into an Excel spreadsheet. You can then use Excel's formulas and functions to perform necessary calculations.

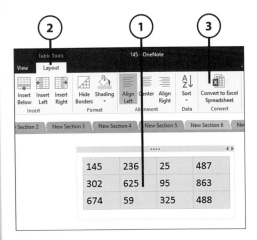

1. Select the table in your notebook or click anywhere in the table.

2. Click or tap the Layout tab.

3. Click or tap Convert to Excel Spreadsheet.

4. A new spreadsheet is now inserted into your notebook, containing the data formerly in the table. You can double-click or double-tap the spreadsheet icon or spreadsheet title to access Excel tools and features.

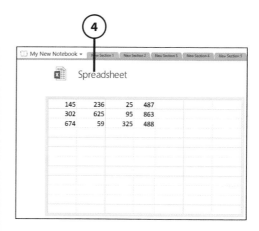

More About Excel

You can tap into Excel's spreadsheet tools and features from within OneNote. Learn more about working with Excel spreadsheets as notes in the next section.

Working with Excel Spreadsheets

Tables are great for displaying simple data, both words and numbers. But when you need to display more complex numeric data, perform calculations on that numeric data, or even display a chart based on that data, you need a spreadsheet. OneNote integrates nicely with Excel for your spreadsheet needs. Microsoft Excel is the spreadsheet application included in Microsoft Office. Designed specifically to help users juggle all kinds of data, particularly numbers, Excel is a powerful part of the Office suite. It works seamlessly alongside OneNote and other Office applications

OneNote lets you embed Excel spreadsheets in your notebooks. You can then use Excel itself to edit and format the embedded spreadsheet. When you select a spreadsheet for editing, you cannot make changes directly in the spreadsheet on your notebook page. Instead, the Excel window opens, along with its tools and features, and you can build and edit spreadsheet data. Any changes you make to the spreadsheet in the Excel window are immediately reflected in the embedded spreadsheet on your notebook page.

Spreadsheet title Embedded spreadsheet Column Excel window

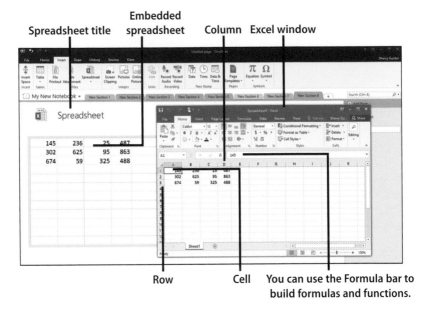

Row Cell You can use the Formula bar to build formulas and functions.

Excel spreadsheets act a lot like tables; you can type in text or numbers, resize columns and rows, add pictures, and so on. Unlike tables, however, you can tap into additional tools for adding formulas and functions, sorting and filtering, and much more. The Excel window uses the same Ribbon-style format to present commands and features, and when you finish working with your spreadsheet, you can return to the OneNote program window and view your spreadsheet as a note element on the notebook page.

Insert a New Spreadsheet

In most instances, you want to create a new spreadsheet in a notebook, and then enter data into that spreadsheet. When you insert a new spreadsheet, you're actually creating it in Microsoft Excel and then linking to it from OneNote.

1. In an open notebook, click or tap where you want to insert the spreadsheet.

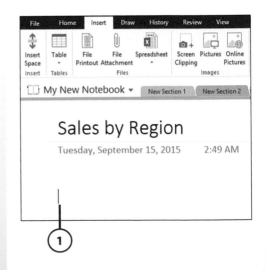

2. Click or tap the Insert tab.

3. Click or tap the Spreadsheet drop-down arrow.

4. Click New Excel Spreadsheet.

5. A new, blank spreadsheet is inserted at the cursor. You can double-click or double-tap the Excel icon to open the Excel window and start editing the spreadsheet.

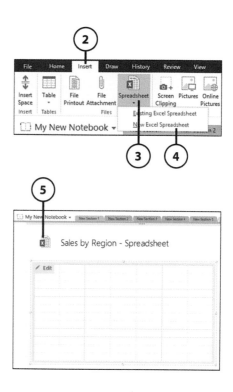

Insert an Existing Spreadsheet

OneNote also lets you embed existing spreadsheets into your notebooks. This is a great way to reference previous work created in Excel.

1. In an open notebook, click or tap where you want to insert the spreadsheet.

2. Click or tap the Insert tab.

3. Click or tap the Spreadsheet drop-down arrow.

4. Click or tap Existing Excel Spreadsheet.

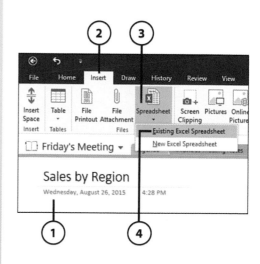

5. Use the Choose Document to Insert dialog box to navigate to and select the spreadsheet you want to insert.

6. Click or tap the Insert button.

7. The Insert File dialog box appears; click or tap Insert Spreadsheet.

8. The spreadsheet is inserted into your notebook; you can double-click or double-tap the Excel icon to open the spreadsheet in the Excel window.

Multiple Sheets

If an inserted spreadsheet has multiple sheets, each sheet appears separately (in order) in your notebook. You can delete sheets you don't want in your notebook.

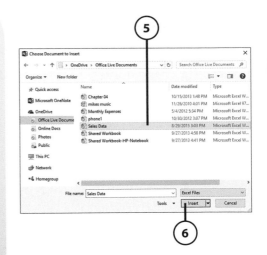

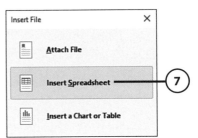

Edit a Spreadsheet

You edit inserted spreadsheets in the Excel window, not in OneNote. So if you want to edit a spreadsheet inserted into a notebook, you have to open that spreadsheet in Excel. However, the OneNote program window remains open, ready for you when you finish with the spreadsheet.

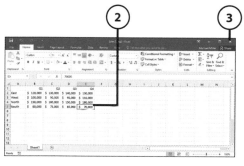

1. Within your notebook, double-click or double-tap the Excel icon or the spreadsheet title to open the spreadsheet in Excel.

2. Enter or edit data within the cells of the spreadsheet.

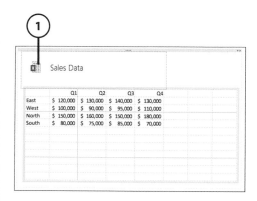

3. When you're done editing the spreadsheet, click or tap the close (X) button in the top-right corner of the Excel window.

4. When prompted to save your changes, click or tap the Save button. The Excel window closes and the spreadsheet in your notebook is updated with the changes you made.

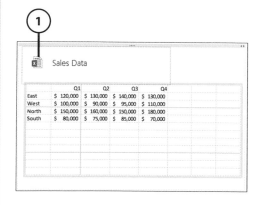

Format a Spreadsheet

Within Excel, you can easily format data in individual cells or the cells themselves. You can use the formatting commands on Excel's Ribbon tabs to edit your spreadsheet data.

1. In your notebook, double-click a spreadsheet to open it in Excel.

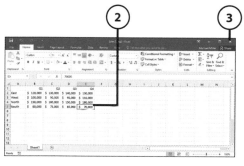

2. Select the cell(s) you want to format.

3. Click or tap the Ribbon's Home tab.

4. Use the controls in the Font group to change font, font size, and font color; bold, italicize, and underline text; add borders around selected cells; and shade cell backgrounds by applying a fill color.

5. Use the controls in the Alignment group to change horizontal (left, center, and right) and vertical (top, middle, and bottom) alignment.

6. Use the controls in the Number group to apply different number formats.

7. Click or tap the Close button to close the Excel window to apply these changes to the spreadsheet in your notebook's embedded spreadsheet.

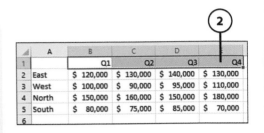

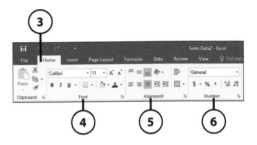

Create a Formula

One of the benefits of using a spreadsheet instead of a table is that you can perform mathematical calculations on the numbers in a spreadsheet by creating a formula within a cell. For example, you can use basic operators in your formulas: + (add), – (subtract), * (multiply), and / (divide).

You start a formula with the equal sign and enter your operations *after* the equal sign. For example, if you want to add 1 plus 2, enter this formula into a cell: **=1+2**. When you press Enter, the formula disappears from the cell—and the result, or *value*, is displayed.

You can perform calculations using values from cells in your spreadsheet by entering the cell location into the formula. For example, if you want to add cells A1 and A2, enter this formula: **=A1+A2**. And if the numbers in either cell A1 or A2 change, the total automatically changes, as well.

1. With your spreadsheet open in the Excel window, select the cell that will contain the formula.

2. Type **=**.

3. Click or tap the first cell you want to include in your formula; that cell location is automatically entered in your formula.

4. Type an operator, such as +, –, *, or /.

5. Click or tap the second cell you want to include in your formula.

6. Repeat steps 4 and 5 to include other cells in your formula, as necessary.

7. Press Enter when your formula is complete.

8. Click to tap the Close button to close the Excel window to view the results of the formula in your notebook.

___

Use the Formula Bar

If you're an experienced Excel user, you can also build formulas directly in the Formula bar. If you ever want to check a cell's formula, click or tap the cell and view the equation in the Formula bar.

___

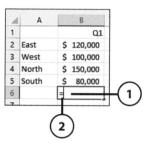

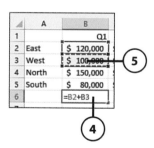

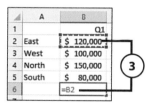

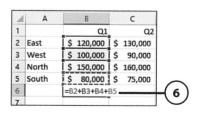

Use Functions

In addition to the basic math operators previously discussed, Excel includes a variety of *functions* that essentially serve as prebuilt formulas. These functions enable you to perform more complex operations. Excel includes hundreds of functions that you can use in your formulas.

You enter a function in the following format: **=function(argument)**, where **function** is the name of the function and **argument** is the range of cells or other data you want to calculate.

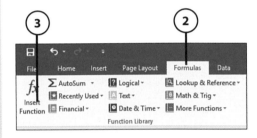

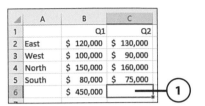

1. With your spreadsheet open in the Excel window, select the cell where you want to insert the function.

2. Click or tap the Formulas tab.

3. Click or tap Insert Function.

4. The Insert Function dialog box opens; click or tap the Or Select a Category drop-down arrow to display the functions of a particular type.

5. Click or tap the function you want to insert.

6. Click or tap OK.

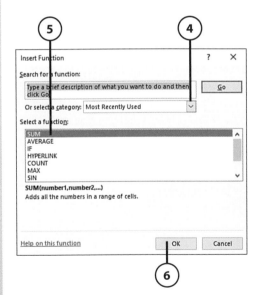

7. If the function has related arguments, a Function Arguments dialog box opens; enter the arguments and click or tap OK. (For example, the first argument may be the range of cells you want to include in the function.) If no arguments are needed, click or tap OK.

8. The function you selected is inserted into the current cell, and the results displayed. (You can view the function and formula in the Formula bar, at the top of the worksheet.)

9. Click or tap the Close button to exit the Excel window and view the results of the function in your notebook.

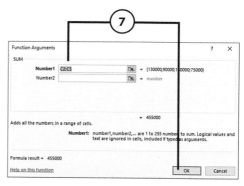

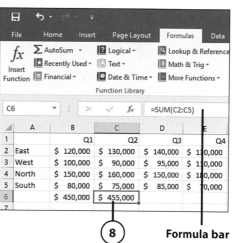

Formula bar

Create a Chart

The numbers you enter into an Excel spreadsheet are often better expressed as a *chart*. A chart can be especially useful when you're referring to your notes, as it visually summarizes more complex numeric data. When you create a chart, the Chart Tools Design tab appears on the Ribbon with tools and features for working with charts.

1. With your spreadsheet open in the Excel window, select the range of cells you want to include in your chart. (If the range has a header row or column, include that row or column when selecting the cells.)

2. Click or tap the Insert tab.

3. Click or tap the button for the category of chart you want to create.

4. Excel displays a variety of charts types in that general category. Click or tap the type of chart you want to create.

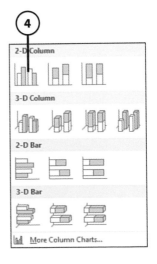

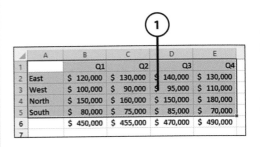

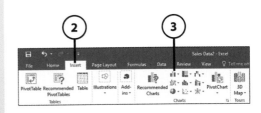

5. When the chart appears in your worksheet, click or tap the Design tab to find tools and features for editing the chart's type, layout, and style.

6. When finished creating your chart, click or tap the Close button to exit the Excel window.

7. The spreadsheet and accompanying chart are now displayed in your notebook.

Learn More

Learn more about Microsoft Excel in the companion book, *My Excel 2016.*

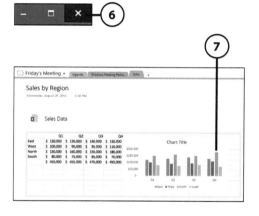

Linked notes in OneNote

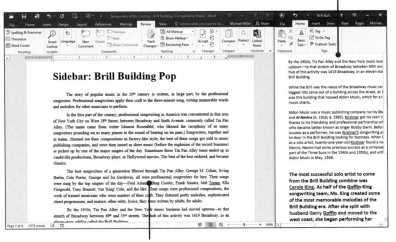

Word document

This chapter shows you how to include in your notebooks links to other notebooks, programs, and web pages. Topics include

→ Linking within OneNote
→ Linking to files and email addresses
→ Linking to content on the Web
→ Managing links
→ Taking linked notes

Working with Links

When you're taking notes with OneNote, you often want to pull in information from various sources, including pages on the Internet. To that end, OneNote lets you insert links to web pages, email addresses, even other pages in OneNote.

You can also use OneNote to create *linked notes* from other programs, such as Microsoft Word or PowerPoint. Linked notes make it easy to do research in other applications; the notes you take in OneNote are automatically linked to whatever you're looking at in Word, PowerPoint, or your Web browser. You can then, at any time, click the link in your OneNote notebook to view the original content in its original location.

Linking Within OneNote

Often, you have notes that refer to other notes taken previously in another notebook location. To make it easier to follow the threads of these notes, you can link to any page or section in your current notebook, or in another notebook.

>>>*Go Further*

EXPLAINING LINKS

A link, or hyperlink, is a selectable reference point that, when clicked, takes you to another source. The source can be another file, a web page, another location in the same document, and so on. The actual link can be just about anything, such as text, a picture, or even an audio or video clip. The most common form of a link is text or a picture.

Text links are easy to spot. Typically, the link text is underlined and sports a brighter color, such as blue. Blue is the most frequent color used for links, and OneNote uses blue by default when you add links to notes. When you click the link text, you jump to another page. You can usually confirm whether text or a picture is a link by hovering your mouse pointer over the link. If the pointer changes from an arrow pointer to a pointing hand icon, you're hovering over a clickable link.

If you do any amount of Web surfing, you're probably used to encountering and using links. Hyperlinks are the essential ingredient of the Web and nearly every web page has links. Links can also be used in documents, or in this case, notebooks. You might insert a link in a note that jumps you to another notebook or takes you to another section in the current notebook. Links are incredibly handy when you're building a notebook that requires cross-referencing with other notes or note information outside of the OneNote 2016 program.

Link to a Page or Section

You can link to individual pages in a notebook, or to larger sections. You can link within the current notebook, or to another notebook created previously. When you review your notes, clicking a link displays the linked-to page or section.

1. Within the current notebook, select the text that you want to link to another section or page.

2. Click or tap the Ribbon's Insert tab.

3. Click or tap Link.

4. The Link dialog box opens; click or tap the + sign next to the notebook you want to link to. This expands the notebook to display available sections and pages.

5. Click the section or page you want to link to.

6. Click OK.

7. The selected text now appears as a link; click or tap the link to activate it and view the original source.

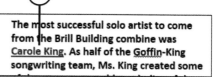

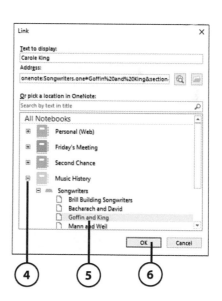

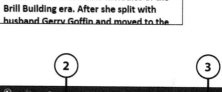

Link to a Specific Paragraph

Sometimes you want to link to a specific paragraph in a notebook. This enables you to go directly to the exact information you need.

1. Open the notebook you want and navigate to the paragraph you want to link to.

2. Right-click (or press and hold if you're using a touchscreen) within this paragraph and select Copy Link to Paragraph.

3. Open or switch to the notebook and section you want to link from.

4. Select the text you want to link from.

5. Click or tap the Insert tab.

6. Click or tap Link.

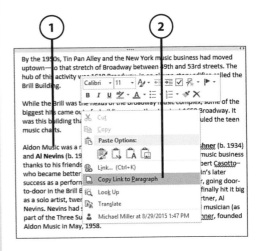

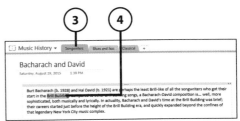

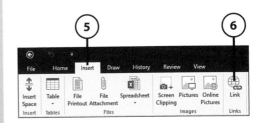

7. The Link dialog box opens; right-click (or press and hold) in the Address box and select Paste.

8. Click OK and the link is added.

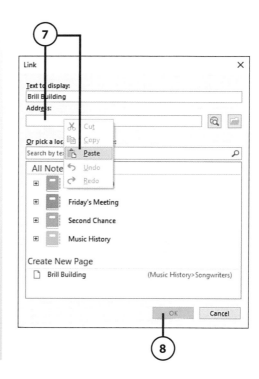

>>>Go Further
CREATE A TABLE OF CONTENTS

If you have a large notebook, you may want to organize it into multiple sections and then create a table of contents for the notebook. You can do this using links to the sections in the notebook.

Create a new page at the beginning of the notebook and title it Table of Contents. Right-click the first page tab after the table of contents and select Copy Link to Section. Place the cursor within the Table of Contents page; then press Ctrl+V. This pastes the name of the page as a hyperlink and creates the first item in your table of contents.

Repeat these steps for the remaining page tabs in your notebook. The result is a table of contents that contains clickable links to every section in your notebook.

Linking to Files and Email Addresses

OneNote enables you to insert links to various types of items into your notes—including files on your computer. You can also insert a link to an email address that, when clicked, opens a new email message to that person.

Link to a File on Your Computer

You can create links to any type of file on your computer—Microsoft Word documents, pictures, music, even videos. When you click on a link to a file, the file is opened in its default application. For example, if you click a link to a Word document, that document is opened in Microsoft Word. If you link to a video file, that video is opened for playback in your default video player app. The file itself is not inserted into your notebook, only a link to that file.

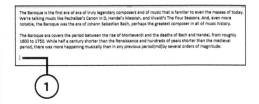

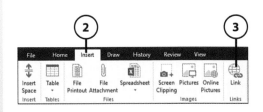

1. Click or tap where you want the link to appear.

2. Click or tap the Insert tab.

3. Click or tap Link.

4. From the Link dialog box, click or tap the Browse for File button.

5. The Link to File dialog box opens; navigate to and select the file you want to link to.

6. Click or tap OK to return to the Link dialog box.

7. The default filename appears in the Text to Display box. You can use the default name or edit the text.

8. Click or tap OK to insert a link to this file in your notebook.

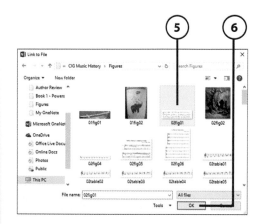

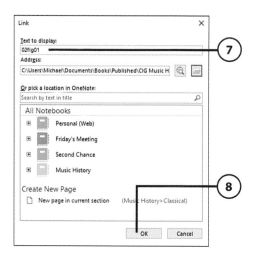

Link to an Email Address

Sometimes your notes may include a person's email address to remind you to contact that person. You can create a live link to any email address, so that when you click on the address, it opens a new email message to that person.

1. Click or tap where you want to insert the email address.

2. Type **mailto:** followed by the email address, like this: **mailto:bob@bob.com**. OneNote immediately turns your text into a link.

Linking to Content on the Web

Much of the research you do takes place on the Internet. Whether you're perusing Wikipedia, using Google to search for specific information, or visiting content-rich websites, the Internet serves the research role previously held by encyclopedias and public libraries. As such, you may want to incorporate content you find on the Web into your OneNote notebooks. There are two ways to do this—link to a given web page or copy a page's content directly into your notes.

Manually Link to a Web Page

The easiest way to reference content found on the Web is to link to that content from within your notebook. When you view your notes, clicking on the link opens your web browser and takes you to the source page.

The easiest way to insert a web page link is to simply type it into your notes.

1. Click or tap where you want the link to appear in your notes.

2. Type the address, like this: **www. webaddress.com/page/**. This automatically creates a hyperlink to the referenced page.

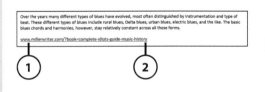

Over the years many different types of blues have evolved, most often distinguished by instrumentation and type of beat. These different types of blues include rural blues, Delta blues, urban blues, electric blues, and the like. The basic blues chords and harmonies, however, stay relatively constant across all these forms.

www.millerwriter.com/?book=complete-idiots-guide-music-history

Copy and Paste

Instead of typing a long web page URL, you can instead copy the page's address from the Address bar in your web browser and then paste it into OneNote.

Link from Existing Text

You can also create a link from exist-ing text in your notebook to any page on the Web.

1. In your notebook, select the text you want to link from.

2. Click or tap the Insert tab.

3. Click or tap Link.

4. In the Link dialog box, type or paste the URL of the page you want to link to into the Address box.

5. Click or tap OK. The selected text is now a hyperlink to the web page you specified.

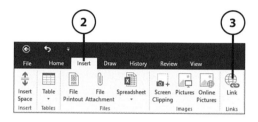

Copy and Paste Linked Web Content

In addition to inserting links to web pages, you can also insert content from web pages into your notes. It's a matter of copying content from a web page and pasting it into a notebook.

1. Open your web browser to the content you want to link and select the text or images you want to copy.

2. Right-click the selected text or images and click or tap Copy.

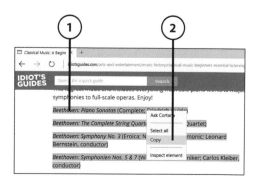

3. In OneNote, position the cursor where you want to paste the web content.

4. On the Ribbon, click or tap the Home tab.

5. Click or tap Paste.

6. The selected text or image is inserted into your notebook, along with a link to the original web page.

7. Click or tap the link to view the source.

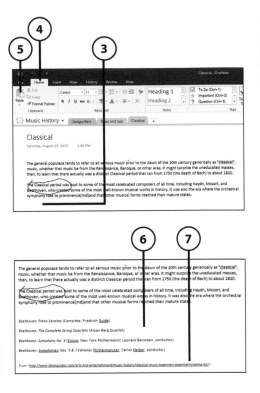

Managing Links

Once you insert any type of link into a notebook, you can go back and edit or delete that link. It's easy to manage links in OneNote.

Edit a Link

What do you do if you try to link to a web page but enter the wrong URL? Or what if you link to an email address and that person's address changes? Easy—edit your link!

1. Right-click or press and hold the link you want to edit.

2. Click or tap Edit Link.

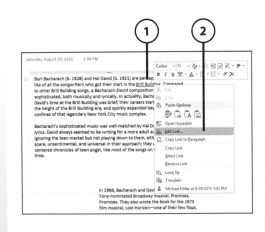

3. Edit the link in the Address box as necessary.

4. Click or tap OK.

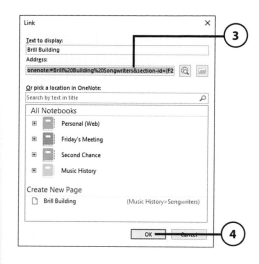

Remove a Link

OneNote lets you remove any link you previously inserted. When you remove a link, the plain note text remains.

1. Right-click or press and hold the link you want to remove.

2. Click or tap Remove Link; OneNote immediately removes the link and restores the original link text formatting.

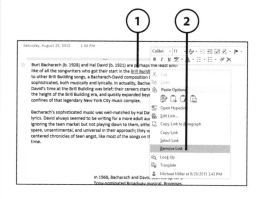

Delete a Link and Link Text

If you want to delete both a link and the text accompanying that link, the process is slightly different.

1. Select the entire text link you want to delete.

Burt Bacharach (b. 1928) and Hal David (b. 1921) are perhaps the least Brill-like of all the songwriters who got their start in the Brill Building. Compared to other Brill Building songs, a Bacharach-David composition is... well, more sophisticated, both musically and lyrically. In actuality, Bacharach and David's time at the Brill Building was brief; their careers started just before the height of the Brill Building era, and quickly expanded beyond the confines of that legendary New York City music complex.

2. Click or tap the Home tab.

3. Click or tap Delete. Alternatively, press the Delete key on your keyboard.

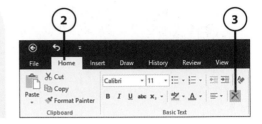

Taking Linked Notes

It's common to take notes while referencing other documents on your computer or pages on the Web. OneNote's linked notes feature enables the notes you take to be automatically linked to the source document.

You activate linked notes from the host application, and a OneNote pane appears docked on the right side of that app window. Enter your notes as normal into the OneNote pane, and they're automatically linked to the document or web page in the other app.

When you refer to these notes later in OneNote, clicking on the notes opens the other application with the document or web page displayed. You no longer have to worry about where your notes were sourced from; the linking is automatic.

You can link notes to Word documents, PowerPoint presentations, and web pages you view in your browser.

Use Linked Notes with Microsoft Word or Microsoft PowerPoint

When you reference content in a Word document or PowerPoint presentation, using linked notes enables you to take notes on that content with OneNote and include links to the original document in your notes.

1. Open the Word document or PowerPoint presentation you want to reference.

2. Click or tap the Review tab.

3. Click or tap the Linked Notes button. This opens a OneNote pane on the right and displays the Select Location in OneNote dialog box.

4. In the dialog box, navigate to and select the notebook and location you want to use. (If you select a section, a new page is created in that section. If you select an existing page, your notes are added to this page.)

5. Click or tap OK.

6. Click or tap in the notes pane and start typing your notes as normal.

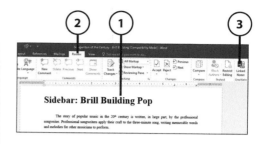

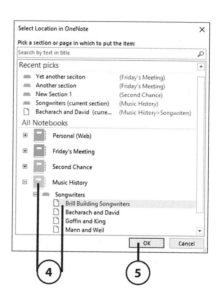

Enabled or Disabled

Linked notes may be started automatically, in which case the chain link icon appears as normal. If the linked notes feature is not yet started (or later stopped), you see a red "no" icon on the chain link icon. You then need to click the chain link icon and click or tap Start Taking Notes to turn the feature on again.

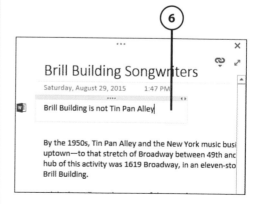

7. An icon appears next to the linked note indicating what app you used for linking, such as a Word or PowerPoint icon.

8. When you're finished taking linked notes, click or tap the chain link icon.

9. Click or tap Stop Taking Linked Notes to turn the feature off.

10. Click or tap the Close button to close the OneNote pane.

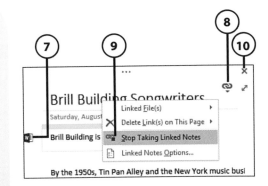

Display the Ribbon

By default, you do not see the Ribbon in the OneNote pane while in linked notes mode. To display the Ribbon, click or tap the More (three dot) icon at the top of the pane.

Use Linked Notes with Internet Explorer

To create linked notes to a given web page, use Microsoft's Internet Explorer browser. When you link notes to Internet Explorer, an IE icon appears next to the OneNote note text.

1. Using Internet Explorer, navigate to the web page you want to reference.

2. Right-click or press and hold in an empty area in the tab row and select Command Bar. This displays the Command bar beneath the Address box.

Other Browsers

OneNote's linked notes feature works only with the Internet Explorer web browser. It does not work with competing Google Chrome or Mozilla Firefox browsers. It also does not work (yet, at least) with the new Microsoft Edge web browser included with Windows 10.

3. In the Command bar, click or tap the OneNote Linked Notes button. This opens a docked OneNote pane on the right and displays the Select Location in OneNote dialog box.

4. In the dialog box, navigate to and select the notebook and location you want to use. (If you select a section, a new page is created in that section. If you select an existing page, your notes are added to this page.)

5. Click or tap OK.

6. Click or tap in the notes pane and start typing your notes as normal.

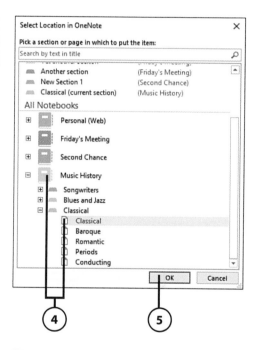

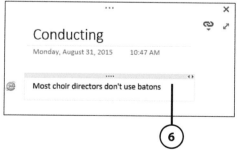

7. To stop taking linked notes, click or tap the chain link icon.

8. Click or tap Stop Taking Linked Notes.

9. Click or tap the Close button to close the OneNote pane.

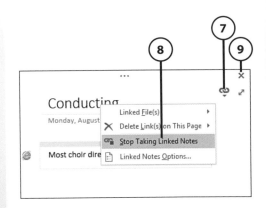

View Linked Notes

You view the notes you take in linked notes mode in your OneNote notebook.

1. Move the mouse pointer over a linked note to view the icon associated with the host application—Microsoft Word, Microsoft PowerPoint, or Internet Explorer.

2. Move the mouse pointer over the application icon to view more details about the referenced document or web page, including the document name.

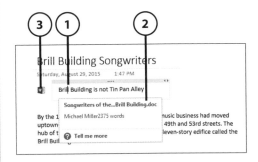

3. Click or tap the application icon to open the host application with the referenced page displayed.

4. To remove the link to the host document, right-click or press and hold the application icon and choose Remove Link.

5. To view a list of files or pages linked to in the current notebook page, click or tap the chain link icon at the top right of the notes page and then click or tap Linked Files.

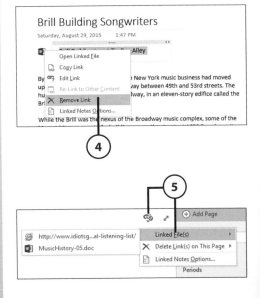

>>>Go Further

USING ONENOTE WITH MICROSOFT EDGE

If your computer is running Microsoft's Windows 10 operating system, you have access to the new Microsoft Edge web browser. Edge replaces Internet Explorer and offers two new ways to work with OneNote.

First, you can easily share any web page directly from Edge to OneNote. In Edge, click or tap the Share button to display the Share pane and then select OneNote. Add any notes on this page to the Add a Note box; then click or tap the drop-down menu at the top to select which notebook section you want to send this to. Click or tap Send to send the web page to OneNote.

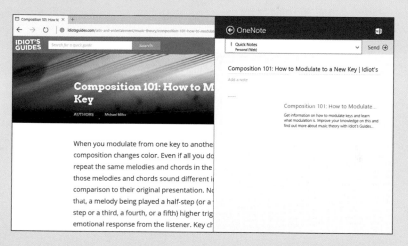

Second, Edge offers a Web Notes mode that lets you mark up a web page with highlights, drawings, and notes. You can then send this marked-up page to OneNote. To enter Web Notes mode, click or tap the Make a Web Note button. Mark up the page as you want and then click or tap the Save button. Click or tap the OneNote tab; then select which notebook section to save to. Click or tap Send and your marked up web page is sent to OneNote.

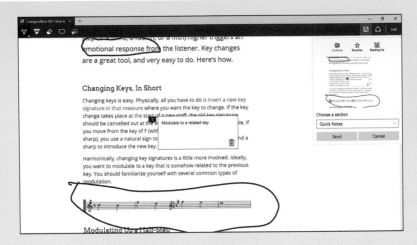

While Edge does not at present enable linked notes to OneNote, these two new sharing options make it easy to share web content—and your notes on that content—with OneNote.

Use the Search box to look through your notes.

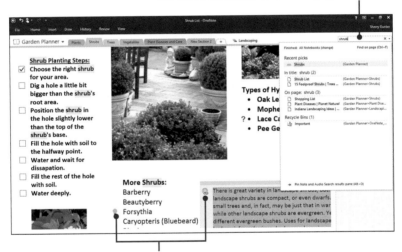

Tags can help you mark notes.

In this chapter, you learn how to use tags to mark notes for special attention, and how to tap into OneNote's powerful search capabilities to look through your notes. Topics include

→ Tagging notes

→ Creating to-do lists

→ Making your own custom tag

→ Pulling together a summary page

→ Searching through notes

Tagging and Searching Notes

If you've ever had to search through a paper notebook for a particular item among pages and pages of notes, you already know what a tedious and time-consuming task it is. Unless you are extremely organized, flipping through pages and skim-reading for the information you are looking for is often fraught with frustration and futility. Thankfully, searching through digital notebooks is fast, intuitive, and pain free. Like many of the Microsoft Office tools, OneNote's search capabilities are powerful and easy to use. Every note you place in a notebook is searchable—even pictures that contain words are searchable. To make searching even easier, you can assign tags to help identify important notes. You never have to dread searching for information again.

Tagging Notes

You can use tags to help you mark important items in your notes, such as identifying a note you need to email or a note you need to add to a To Do list. When you assign a tag to a note, an icon typically appears in the top-left corner of the note, or in the case of pictures, on the left-hand side of the image. To view a tag, just move the mouse pointer over the tag icon to reveal a pop-up ScreenTip with the name of the tag. Some tags involve highlighting rather than icons. If you apply the Remember for Later tag, for example, a yellow highlight appears on the note.

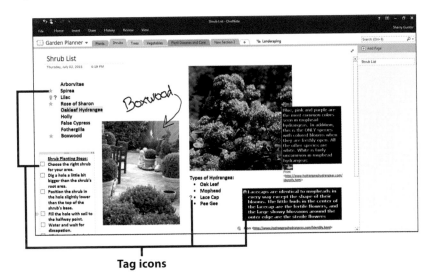

Tag icons

Tags are a great way to identify items that need special attention or action. As if this isn't enough reason to use tags, here's a big one—you can use tags to search notes. OneNote's tagging feature includes the capability to compile all the tagged notes in one spot for easy access, lookup, and printout. For example, let's say you're working on a research project. You can tag all the notes pertaining to a certain subject with a distinct tag. Later, when you need to reference all those notes, you can search for the tag. OneNote displays a Tags Summary pane with all the tags for a particular notebook, section, or group.

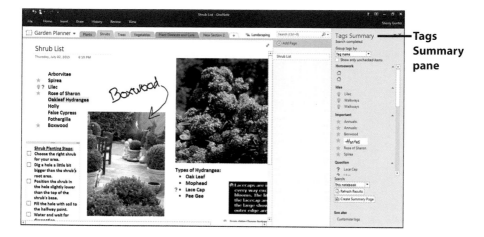

OneNote includes a library of preset tags you can choose from or you can create your own customized tags. Here are just a few of the preset tags you can assign:

- To Do
- Important
- Question
- Remember for later
- Definition
- Highlight
- Contact
- Address
- Phone number
- Web site to visit
- Idea
- Schedule meeting
- Send in email
- Call back
- Book to read
- Movie to see
- Music to listen to
- Source for article
- Critical

If the preset tags don't meet your needs, you can create your own tags to use with your notes. For example, if you're working on a research paper, you may need to create some tags related to topics you're covering. If you're using a notebook for a work project, you might need to create some task-specific tags. You can create new tags or modify existing ones in OneNote, and use the Customize Tags dialog box to manage them all.

Customize Tags
dialog box

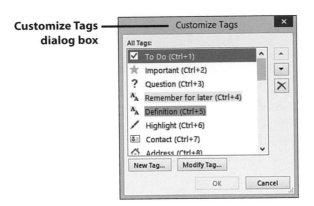

You can assign multiple tags to a note, up to nine per note. OneNote tags hang out on the Ribbon's Home tab. You can find a list of tags to choose from in a gallery box. You can also access tags through a shortcut menu when you right-click or press and hold over a note.

If you find yourself using the same tag over and over again, you might want to memorize its keyboard shortcut command so you can easily assign it with just a simple key press. For example, to apply the To Do tag, press Ctrl+1. When viewing the list of tags in the Ribbon's gallery box, keyboard shortcut keys appear next to the first nine tags listed.

Tags menu

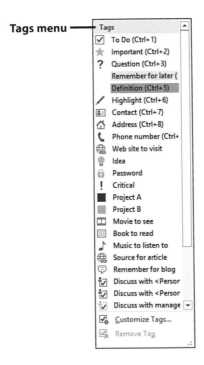

Assign a Tag

You can use the Ribbon's Home tab to assign tags to your notes. You can assign tags to text notes, pictures, audio and video notes, and more. You can also assign multiple tags to the same notebook item.

1. Click or tap the note item you want to assign a tag to, or click or tap in front of the line of text you want to mark.

2. Click or tap Home.

3. Peruse the tags available in the Tags gallery; click or tap the scroll arrows to scroll through the list.

4. Click or tap the More button to view the entire list.

5. Click or tap the tag you want to assign.

Tagging Handwriting

You can tag things you write or draw with a stylus on touchscreen devices. Click or tap the hand-writing or drawing and choose Tag from the pop-up toolbar. OneNote displays the tag menu list; click or tap a tag to assign it.

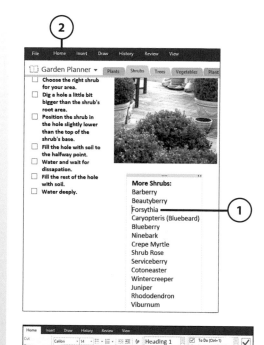

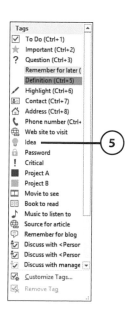

6. OneNote places a tag icon next to the note.

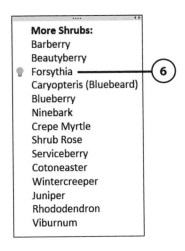

More Shrubs:
Barberry
Beautyberry
Forsythia ——————— 6
Caryopteris (Bluebeard)
Blueberry
Ninebark
Crepe Myrtle
Shrub Rose
Serviceberry
Cotoneaster
Wintercreeper
Juniper
Rhododendron
Viburnum

Make a Checklist with the To Do Tag

The To Do tag is special; it adds a check box next to the note. You can use it to mark pending activities and check them off when they're complete. You can also use the To Do tag to create a checklist, such as errands you need to run or daily tasks you need to do. In this example, the To Do tag is applied to create a checklist.

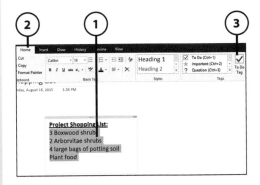

1. Select the note or note text you want to assign a check box to.

2. Click or tap Home.

3. Click or tap To Do Tag.

4. OneNote inserts check boxes in front of each item.

5. Click or tap a check box to mark the item as completed.

Project Shopping List:
☐ 3 Boxwood shrubs
☐ 2 Arborvitae shrubs
☐ 4 large bags of potting soil
☑ Plant food

Tagging for Outlook Tasks

You can turn any note text into an automatic To Do list task in Microsoft Outlook using the Outlook Tasks menu button. This button is only available on the Home tab or Mini toolbar if you have Outlook installed. Click or tap the Outlook Tasks button and choose the type of task reminder you want to apply. OneNote adds a flag to mark the text. When you switch over to Outlook, you can see the newly added tasks in the To Do list.

List as You Go

You can also assign a To Do tag before you ever type in a list. Activate the To Do Tag command and type in the first list item. When you press Enter/Return, OneNote automatically adds another blank check box and you can continue typing in the list items. When you get to the end of your list, press Enter twice to turn off the To Do Tag command.

Try a Template

OneNote includes several page templates designed just for To Do lists. To assign a To Do List template, click or tap the Insert tab on the Ribbon, display the Page Templates drop-down list, and click or tap Page Templates. This opens the Templates pane. Look for the To Do List templates under the Planners category.

>>>Go Further

CONTROLLING YOUR TO DO LIST

You can manage your To Do lists in OneNote in several ways. Of course, the check marks are an obvious action; you can select or deselect the check boxes to mark items as done or not done. You can also control the list's hierarchy and create subtasks. For example, if you're creating a list of projects to do around the house, you may end up with several main projects that require sublists of minor details to check off before the entire project is complete. You can make subtasks under main tasks, or "master" tasks. Just press the Tab key to start a subtask under a main list task.

You can also move tasks up or down in your To Do list to change their order. One of the easy ways to do this is using the keyboard. Click or tap the task and then press Alt+Shift+Up Arrow on the keyboard to move a task up in the list order, or press Alt+Shift+Down Arrow to move a task down in the list. If you prefer using a mouse or touchscreen, you can also click and drag or tap and drag the task and drop it elsewhere in the list to move it.

Delete a Tag

You can remove tags you no longer want associated with a note. When you activate the Remove Tag command, OneNote removes all the tags for the note or tagged text.

1. Click or tap the tagged item.

2. Click or tap Home.

3. Display the Tags menu list.

4. Click or tap Remove Tag.

5. OneNote removes the tag or tags.

Removal Shortcut

You can also right-click or press and hold the tag icon and choose Remove Tag to delete the tag.

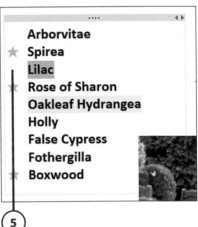

Modify a Tag

You can make modifications to a tag to change its name, icon, font, or highlight color. Editing an existing tag is handy if you only need to make slight adjustments, such as changing a tag color for different notebook users.

1. Click or tap Home.

2. Click or tap the Tag gallery's More button.

3. Click or tap Customize Tags.

4. Click or tap the tag you want to edit.

5. Click or tap Modify Tag.

6. To change the tag's name, type a new name here.

7. To change the icon associated with the tag, click or tap the Symbol list button and choose another icon.

More Edits

You can always make more changes to a tag later. Just revisit the Customize Tags dialog box, choose the tag to edit, and click or tap Modify Tag again.

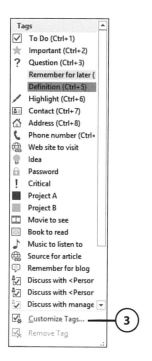

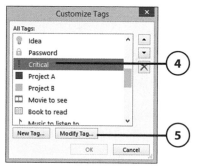

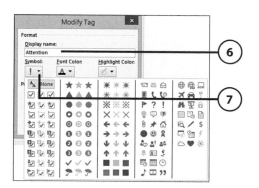

8. To change the font color, click or tap Font Color and choose another color.

9. To change the highlight color or assign a highlight color, click or tap Highlight Color and choose a color from the pop-up list.

10. Click OK.

11. OneNote updates the tag in the list and any existing tags on the page update as well. Click OK to save your changes.

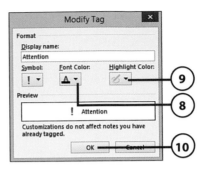

Create a Custom Tag

You can create a brand new tag for your notebook using the Customize Tags dialog box. When creating a new tag, you pick a name, icon, and font or highlight color for the tag. The new tag is added to the tags menu list.

1. Click or tap Home.

2. Click or tap the Tag gallery's More button.

3. Click or tap Customize Tags.

4. Click or tap New Tag.

5. Type a name for the new tag.

6. Click or tap the Symbol button and choose an icon.

7. If you want a different font color for the tag, click or tap Font Color and choose a color.

8. Optionally, click or tap Highlight Color if you want to assign a highlight color to the tag.

9. Click OK.

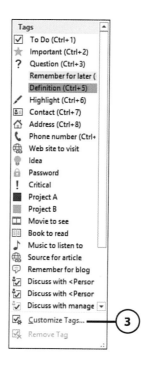

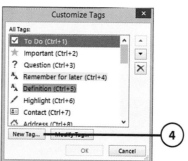

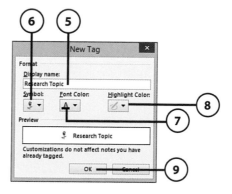

10. OneNote adds the tag to the top of the list. Click OK to save your changes and exit the Customize Tags dialog box.

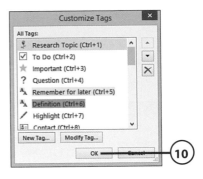

Find Tags

It's easy to find a tagged note using the Tags Summary pane. For example, if you marked a note in your notebook with the Important tag, you can quickly see where the tag is located and view it right away.

1. Click or tap Home.

2. Click or tap Find Tags.

3. The Tags Summary pane opens; click or tap the tag you want to view to jump right to the tag in the notebook.

4. If the pane displays a long list of tags, you can expand and collapse the tag groups; click or tap an Expand/Collapse icon.

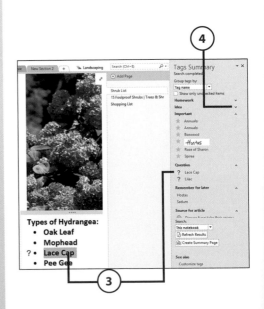

5. By default, the Tags Summary page lists tags by name. To choose another sort type, click or tap the Group Tags By drop-down arrow and choose a filter.

6. To search in specific sections, notebooks, or all notebooks, click or tap the Search drop-down arrow and choose where you want to search for tags.

7. Click or tap Close to close the Tags Summary pane.

Leave It Open

You can leave the Tags Summary pane open as long as you need to as you're working with tags. If you make changes to any tags on a page, you can click or tap the Refresh Results button in the Tags Summary pane to update the list of tags shown in the pane.

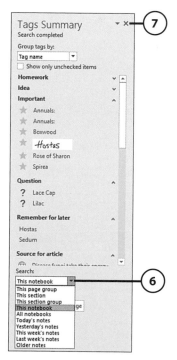

Create a Summary Page

You can create a page in your note-book that summarizes your tagged notes. Called a summary page, this is a list of your tags across pages and sections in your notebook. You can specify which type of tags to summarize.

1. Click or tap Home.

2. Click or tap Find Tags.

3. Click or tap Create Summary Page.

4. OneNote inserts a new page in the current section.

5. Click or tap here and type a new name for the page.

6. To view a particular tag in its original location, click or tap the tag icon and then click or tap the Notebook icon that appears.

Print It

To print your summary page, click or tap the File menu on the Ribbon, and then click or tap Print to view print options. To print the page, click or tap Print.

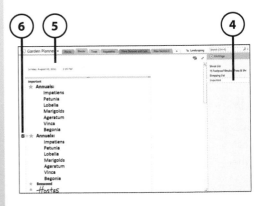

Searching Through Notes

It's easy to search through your notes. A handy Search box is just waiting for you in the upper-right corner of the OneNote program window. You can use the Search box to type in keywords and phrases, or *search strings* (a combination of characters and words you're searching for). The Search box includes a Change Search Scope drop-down arrow that allows you to control where the search takes place. You can search just the current page, a section, the entire notebook, or all the notebooks you've created. By default, the search feature is set up to search all notebooks unless you specify otherwise.

Search Results list   **Search box**   **Change Search Scope menu arrow**

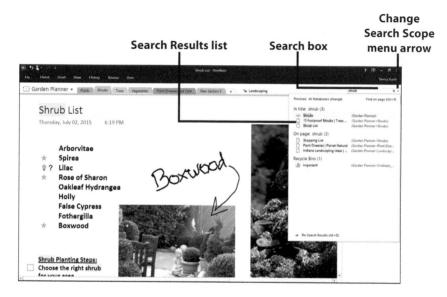

OneNote can search not only text notes, but also handwritten notes. Thanks to handwriting recognition, OneNote can decipher your handwriting, and with optical character recognition (OCR), OneNote can also search for text within images.

Search Through All Notebooks

By default, OneNote is set up to search through all your notebooks when you use the Search box.

1. Click or tap the Search box.

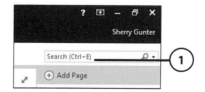

2. Type in the text you want to search for, whether it's a single word or an entire phrase.

3. The Search Results list immediately shows any matching results; click or tap a match.

4. OneNote jumps to the matching text and highlights it in your notes.

5. The Search Results list remains open in case you want to check out another match. Press Esc or click or tap anywhere outside the results list when finished.

Pin the Search Results

You can pin the Search Results list onscreen so it's in view as long as you need it. Just click or tap the Pin Search Results command at the bottom of the list, or press Alt+O on the keyboard.

Shortcut

You can also use a keyboard shortcut to search through all your notebooks. Press Ctrl+E on the keyboard to open the Search pane and activate the Search box; type your search text and press Enter.

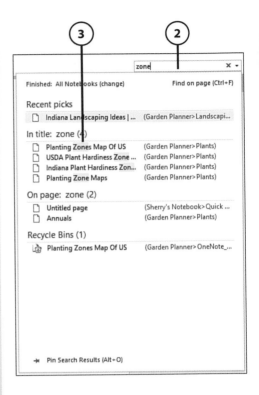

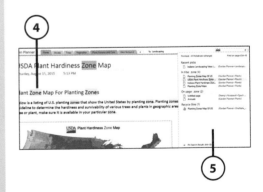

Narrow the Search Scope

If you want to search through the current notebook you're using, you can change the scope of the search with the Change Search Scope menu. You can use the Change Search Scope setting to search a particular section, group, or current notebook.

1. Click or tap the Change Search Scope drop-down arrow at the right end of the Search box.

2. Click or tap This Section.

3. Type in the text you want to search for, whether it's a single word or an entire phrase.

4. The Search Results list immediately shows any matching results; click or tap a match.

5. OneNote jumps to the matching text and highlights it in your notes.

Change the Default

If you prefer to use the same search scope each time, such as This Section or This Notebook, you can set it as the default search scope. Click or tap the Change Search Scope arrow and choose your search type. Next, click or tap the menu again and choose Set This Scope as Default.

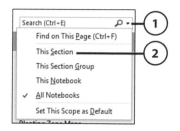

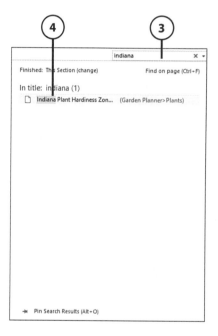

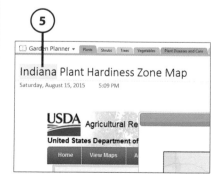

6. The Search Results list remains open in case you want to check out another match; when finished, press Esc.

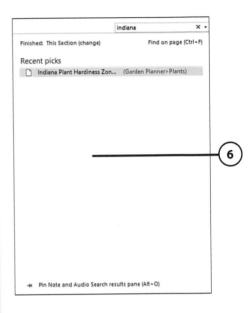

Search through Audio and Video Clips

You can also search for spoken words found in audio or video clip notes. This feature works only if you turn on the Audio Search tool. By default, this tool is not activated since it slows down the search action. You can turn the feature on when you need it and turn it off when you don't. These steps explain how to activate the Audio Search tool.

1. Click or tap File.

2. Click or tap Options.

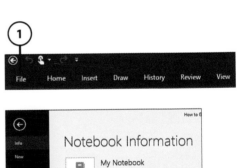

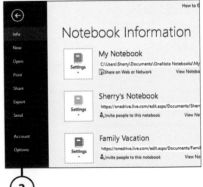

3. Click or tap Audio & Video.

4. Under the Audio Search section, click or tap the check box in front of Enable Searching Audio and Video Recordings for Words option.

5. The Audio Search prompt box appears warning you that an audio search may take awhile; click Enable Audio Search to continue.

6. Click OK.

7. Type in the text you want to search for, whether it's a single word or an entire phrase.

8. The Search Results lists matching results; any audio and video results are noted by the appearance of the Audio & Video Playback tab on the Ribbon.

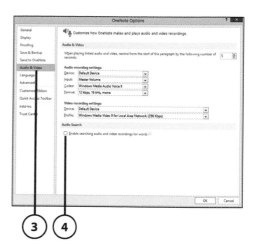

9. Click or tap Playback to view playback controls.

10. Click or tap Play to play the clip.

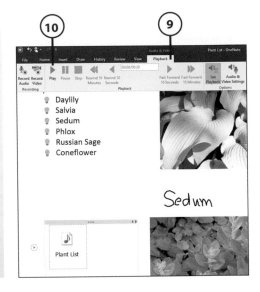

>>>Go Further

PATIENCE COUNTS

If you've recorded several long audio or video clips as notes, it may take awhile to search through them for the search keywords you specified. Be patient. The audio recognition process can take at least twice as much time as the length of the recording. Because the audio and video search is so slow, the feature is disabled by default so it doesn't slow down regular text searches.

Turn It Off Again

When you finish searching through audio and video notes, it's a good idea to return to the OneNote Options dialog box and disable the audio feature again.

Use the built-in Thesaurus tool to look up synonyms and antonyms.

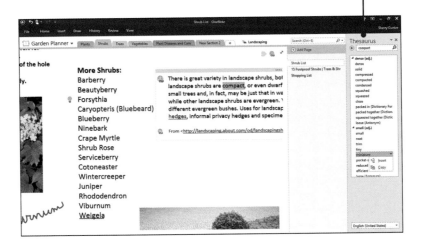

In this chapter, you find out how to use OneNote's research and reviewing tools. Topics include

→ Checking your pages for misspelled words
→ Adding your own typos to AutoCorrect
→ Looking up synonyms with the Thesaurus
→ Translating note text

Researching and Reviewing with OneNote

OneNote includes several features to assist you with researching and reviewing your notes. As part of the overall goal of helping you organize your thoughts, ideas, and notations, it's not surprising that OneNote includes tools for checking translations, looking up definitions, and checking spelling and grammar, just to name a few. Microsoft has provided research option services for several years now with the Office suite. With OneNote 2016, you have access to these tools through the Research task pane and the Ribbon's Review tab. As you learn in this chapter, OneNote makes it easy to keep on top of your note-taking tasks with specialized tools for researching and reviewing your work.

Using the Spell Checking Tools

Spell checking is one of the best tools ever created for the world of computing, especially for users who share their work with others. It's an embedded program that runs from within other programs, such as OneNote, to flag words that may not be spelled correctly. Spell checking tools are common among programs that use a lot of text-based input. Basically, a spell checker scans text and compares it with a dictionary of known entries. If it detects an unknown spelling, it alerts you to the possible error. It's up to you to fix the spelling issue or ignore it. You can run the Spelling tool in OneNote any time you want to check your notebook for spelling and grammar problems.

OneNote's Spelling tool opens a Spelling pane as it checks your text. When something is amiss, the Spelling tool highlights the issue in your note text as well as in the Spelling pane. A red, wavy line indicates a possible spelling problem. The Spelling pane offers you several options for dealing with the issue. You can change the spelling or you can ignore it. If the word is spelled correctly, such as a proper name or specialized terminology, you can choose to add it to the dictionary so the Spelling tool doesn't view it as a discrepancy.

Highlighted text   **Spelling pane**

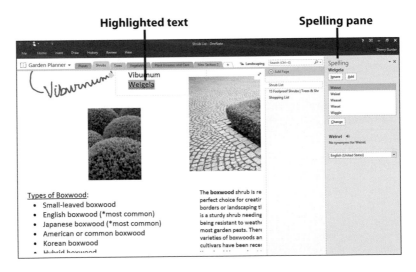

Many programs also utilize an automatic spell check that works as you type. Called AutoCorrect in the Microsoft Office suite, this feature automatically corrects typos for you as you're tapping away at the keyboard or offers suggestions for possible spellings. For example, let's say you're busy typing and begin to type in the word "the" but accidentally switch the "h" and the "e" around. Instead of leaving the word as "teh," AutoCorrect fixes it immediately, changing it to "the." Most of the time, you may not even notice the correction. AutoCorrect works seamlessly in the background guessing at what you're typing. If it encounters a not-so-common misspelling, it underlines the word in a red, wavy line. You can right-click or press and hold the word to reveal a pop-up menu of suggestions and correction options. These are the same options found in the Spelling pane.

Underlined word ——

Shortcut menu

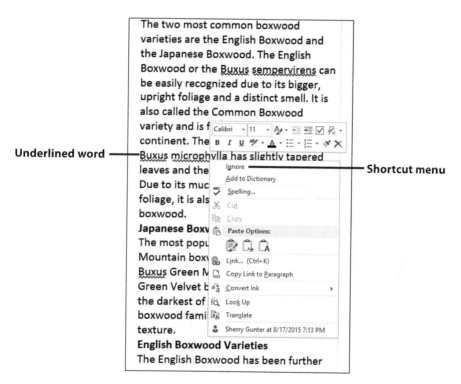

By default, AutoCorrect is turned on in OneNote unless you choose to turn it off. You can control all of the program's spelling features through OneNote's Options dialog box. The Options dialog box has a whole section of settings for proofing your work. Many of the settings are turned on by default; however, you can make changes to these settings to suit the way you work.

Proofing settings **Autocorrect options**

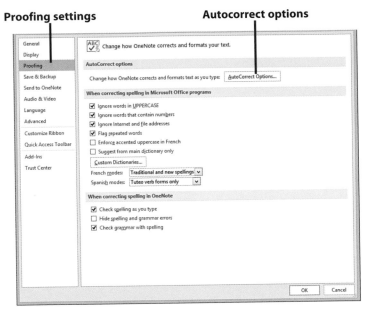

Check Spelling

You can run a spell check on your entire notebook page to check for issues or just use it to check a single note. When the Spelling tool finds a potential problem, it's highlighted in the note and in the Spelling pane. As you address each issue, the Spelling tool moves on to the next until it reaches the end of the page.

1. Click or tap the top of the page, or click or tap where you want the spell check to start.

2. Click or tap the Ribbon's Review tab.

3. Click or tap Spelling.

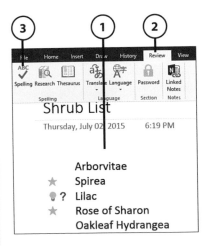

4. OneNote opens the Spelling pane and lists any found spelling issues, as well as highlights misspelled text.

5. To change the spelling, click or tap a revised spelling from the list of options and click or tap Change.

6. To ignore the misspelling, click or tap Ignore.

7. To add the word to the built-in dictionary, click or tap Add.

8. When the end of the spell check is complete, click or tap OK.

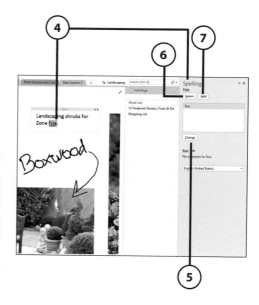

Stop the Spell Check

You can choose to stop the spell check at any time by simply closing the Spelling pane. Click or tap the pane's Close button.

Check Again

If you run a complete spell check, you can't run it again unless you make changes to text on the page.

Turn Off Automatic Spell Checking

If you prefer not to have your spelling and grammar checked as you type, you can turn off the feature. All the proofing settings are found in the OneNote Options dialog box.

1. Click or tap the File tab on the Ribbon.

2. Click or tap Options.

3. Click or tap Proofing.

4. Deselect the Check Spelling as You Type check box to turn off the feature.

5. Deselect the Check Grammar with Spelling check box to turn off the grammar checking tool.

6. Click OK.

Turn It On Again

To turn the automatic spell checking and grammar checking on again, simply open the OneNote Options dialog and check the two settings again.

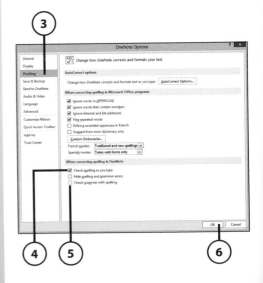

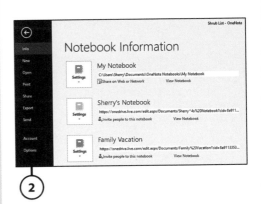

Add Your Own Typos to AutoCorrect

AutoCorrect fixes spelling errors for you automatically as you type. It uses a list of commonly misspelled words, and you can add your own favorite typos to the list.

1. Click or tap the File tab on the Ribbon.

2. Click or tap Options.

3. Click or tap Proofing.

4. Click or tap AutoCorrect Options.

5. To add your own commonly misspelled word to the list, click or tap the Replace box and type it just as you typically misspell it.

6. Click or tap the With box and type in the correction.

7. Click or tap Add.

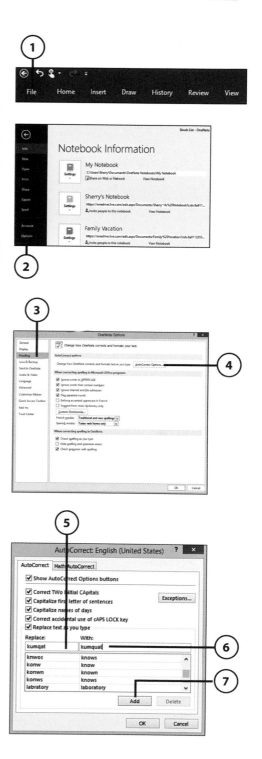

8. Click or tap OK to exit the dialog box.

9. Click or tap OK to close the OneNote Options dialog box.

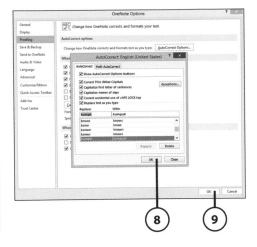

>>>Go Further

SAVE TIME WITH AUTOCORRECT

If you find yourself typing in a long company name or similar phrase over and over again, you can turn it into an AutoCorrect entry. Designate an abbreviation for the name and the next time you type in the abbreviation, AutoCorrect substitutes the full name. This can be a real time saver for names, phrases, and special symbols you constantly use in your notebooks.

To add a name or phrase, open the AutoCorrect dialog box as detailed in the previous steps. In the Replace box, type in the abbreviation you want to use. In the With box, type in the full name you want to swap the abbreviation for; then click or tap Add.

You can also remove words from the AutoCorrect list. Simply select the word from the list and click or tap the Delete button.

Using the Thesaurus

As you're proofreading your notes, you may find yourself using the same word over and over again and it's becoming redundant. You can use OneNote's Thesaurus tool to look up *synonyms*—words that mean the same thing as another word. Part of several reviewing tools in OneNote, the Thesaurus pane lets you enter words and look up similar meanings. You can also select a word in your notes and display synonyms from which to replace it. The Thesaurus tool lets you look up both synonyms and antonyms (words that mean the opposite). This tool is particularly helpful if you want to add more variety to your note-writing tasks. As with other panes in OneNote, you can keep the Thesaurus pane open as long as you need and close it when you finish working with it.

Antonym   Synonyms   Thesaurus pane

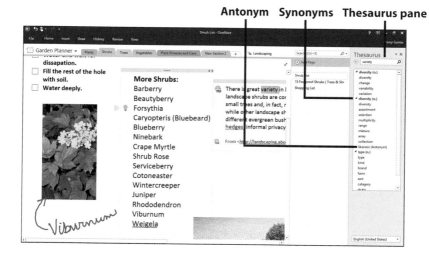

Look Up a Synonym

You can use the Thesaurus tool to look up a synonym. The Thesaurus pane displays a list of synonyms and antonyms.

1. Select the word you want to look up.

2. Click or tap Review.

3. Click or tap Thesaurus.

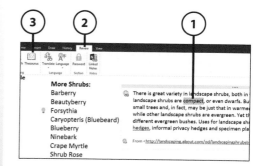

4. Move the mouse pointer over the word you want to use; click or tap the drop-down arrow that appears.

5. Click or tap Insert to replace the selected word with the synonym.

6. Click or tap Close to close the Thesaurus pane.

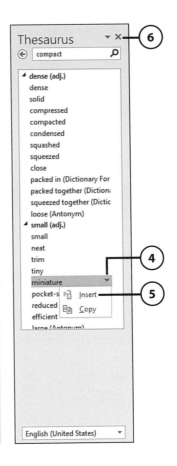

Using the Research Task Pane

You can use OneNote's Research task pane to look for information from a set of online resources. The Research task pane is featured in all the Microsoft Office programs. It offers access to a variety of reference books, translation services, and research sites. From the Research pane, you can look up words and phrases using the Encarta Dictionary and Thesaurus (English, French, and Spanish) as well as translation tools using the Bilingual Dictionary. You can also search through a variety of online services, such as Bing, Factiva iWorks, Merriam-Webster, and much more. To use any of these services or sources, however, you must have an online connection.

Research pane   **List of online research services**

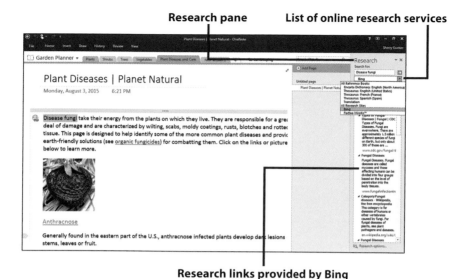

Research links provided by Bing

The Bing site is the default service used in the Research task pane, and it also happens to be Microsoft's primary search engine of choice. Factiva iWorks (a third-party information service) is another option available, focusing on business information. Use it to look for publications, news stories, or photos related to your research. Both of these Internet research websites offer you quick access to a wealth of online information without needing to open a separate browser window. If you have another service you prefer to use, you can add it to the list. The more services you add, the more results appear in the Research task pane.

Open the Research Task Pane

Use the Research task pane to look up information online using the Microsoft Office research tools. You can conduct a quick search for topics, words, or phrases using Bing, Factiva iWorks, the Encarta Dictionary, or several language thesauruses.

1. Select the word or phrase you want to research.

2. Click or tap Review.

3. Click or tap Research.

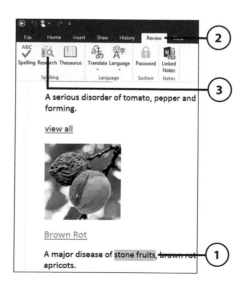

4. The Research pane displays matching results; you can click or tap a link to open your web browser and read more about the information.

5. Use the scroll arrows to view various entries.

6. Click or tap the drop-down arrow to switch services.

7. To look up another word or phrase, type here and press Enter/Return.

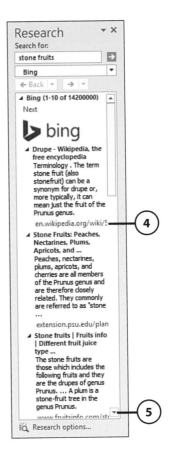

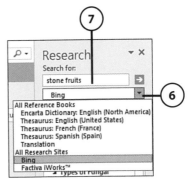

8. Scroll to the bottom of the pane to view additional options.

9. Click or tap Close to close the Research pane.

Change Search Services

You can turn search services on or off, or add new ones to the Research task pane. To add a service, you need the search provider's web address.

1. With the Research task pane open, click or tap Research options at the bottom of the pane.

2. The Research Options dialog box opens; click or tap a check box to select or deselect a service (a check mark indicates the service is selected).

3. Optionally, to add a service, click or tap here and enter the web address.

4. Click or tap OK to exit the dialog box.

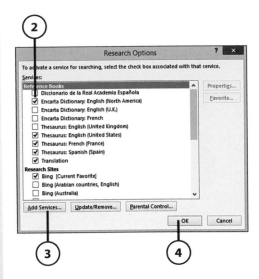

Internet Research Sites

There are many Internet research services, some of which are free. Most, however, require a subscription to use their services. Be sure to check out the service thoroughly before committing to a subscription plan.

Translating Text

You can translate words and phrases in your notes and specify which language to use. Tapping into the powerful Microsoft Office translation tools, you can easily decipher text in other languages or turn your current language into a note someone else can understand.

Two translation options are available through the Translate command on the Review tab:

Translate Selected Text   Use this feature to translate a paragraph, sentence, or phrase.

Mini Translator   Use this tool to quickly view a word's translation simply by pointing at it with your cursor, with your finger or stylus (touchscreen users).

You can also set a proofing language and OneNote remembers your choice the next time you run a spell check.

The translation tools work in conjunction with the Research pane, allowing you to change languages as well as view translations.

The Mini Translator displays a pop-up box for words on the notebook page.

The Research pane is also used for translation tasks.

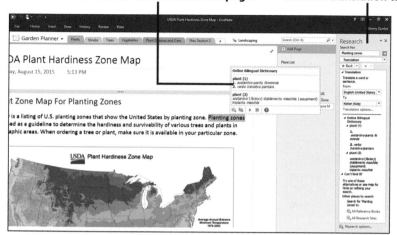

Translate Selected Text

With an Internet connection, you can easily translate text from within OneNote using the Research pane. You can specify which language and choose either the Microsoft Translator service or another third-party service.

1. Select the text you want to translate.

2. Click or tap Review.

3. Click or tap Translate.

4. Click or tap Translate Selected Text.

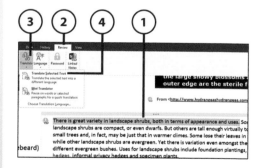

5. A prompt box appears; click or tap Yes to proceed.

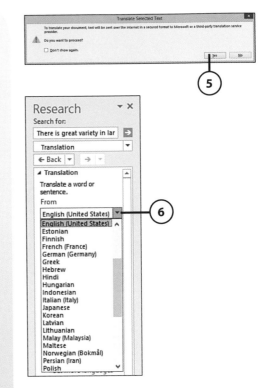

6. Click or tap From and choose a language.

7. Click or tap To and choose a language.

More Translation Languages

You can click or tap the Translation options link in the Research pane to open the Translation Options dialog box and choose from additional languages.

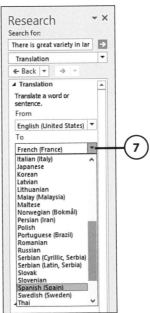

8. The selected text is translated.

9. To insert the text into your note to replace the selected text, click or tap the Insert button and choose Insert.

10. Click or tap the Close button to exit the Research pane.

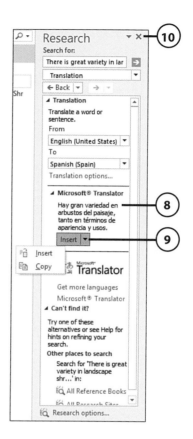

Set a Proofing Language

You can also control which language OneNote recognizes for handwriting and proofing tools. Click or tap the Review tab, click or tap Languages, and choose Set Proofing Language. This opens the Proofing Tools pane where you can select a language.

>>>Go Further
CHANGE LANGUAGE PREFERENCES

You can specify a language for display buttons, tabs, and the Help files using OneNote's language preferences settings. Click or tap the Review tab, click or tap Languages, and choose Language Preferences. This opens the OneNote Options dialog box to the Language settings. You can choose an editing language or a display language to use in OneNote. For example, if you prefer using French, you can set the display language to French, and OneNote displays the commands and buttons in French. You can even set a language as the default so it's used every time you open OneNote.

Use the Mini Translator

You can use the Mini Translator tool to quickly translate a word on your notebook page. You can specify which language to use with the translation. Whenever you pause the mouse over a word, a faint pop-up box appears, and when you move the mouse over the box you can view the translation.

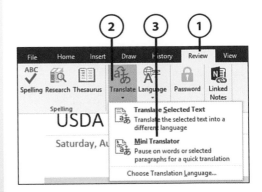

1. Click or tap Review.

2. Click or tap Translate.

3. Click or tap Mini Translator.

4. The Translation Language Options dialog box opens the first time you use this feature; click or tap the Translate To menu and choose a language.

5. Click or tap OK.

6. Hover the mouse over a word you want to translate.

7. A very faint pop-up box displays the translation; move the mouse over the box to view the translation.

8. Optionally, if you want to display the translation in the Research task pane, you can click or tap the Expand icon.

9. You can click or tap the Play icon to hear an audio translation.

10. Move the mouse pointer off the pop-up box to make it disappear.

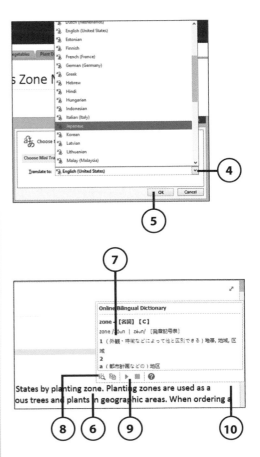

Turn It Off

The Mini Translator remains on until you choose to toggle it off again. To turn off the Mini Translator, click or tap the Review tab, click or tap Translator, and select Mini Translator.

Change the Language

To change the translation language used, click or tap the Review tab, click or tap Translator, and then click or tap Choose Translation Language. You can then select another language from the Translation Language Options dialog box.

OneNote sharing options

This chapter describes how to share your notes and notebooks with others. Topics include

→ Printing notes
→ Exporting notes
→ Emailing notes
→ Sharing notebooks

Distributing and Sharing Notes

Sometimes you work by yourself. Other times you work with other people. When you want to share your notes with others, OneNote offers several different ways to do so. You can go the old school route and print out your notes. You can export your notes into Word or PDF documents for sharing distribution. You can also email your notes to friends and coworkers. You can even share your notebooks with coworkers, so they can view or edit them directly at their leisure. In this chapter, you'll learn about the various ways to share and distribute your notebooks and notes.

Printing Notes

We start with the most basic and perhaps easiest way to share your notes—by printing them on your printer. Some people like to have printed copies of their notes and even take additional handwritten notes on those printed copies. OneNote's printing options let you print entire notebooks, or specified sections or pages.

Print Sections of a Notebook

You can choose to print a single page, group of pages, or entire section of a notebook.

1. Click or tap the File tab.

2. Click or tap Print to display print options.

3. Click or tap Print Preview to display the Print Preview and Settings dialog box.

4. Click or tap the Print Range drop-down arrow to select what part of your notebook you want to print: Page Group, Current Page, or Current Section.

5. To print on something different from standard letter size paper, click or tap the Paper Size drop-down arrow and make a new selection.

6. To fit your notes to the width of the page, click or tap to check the Scale Content to Paper Width option. (This is probably checked by default.)

7. In the Orientation section, click or tap either Portrait or Landscape.

8. To add a footer to the printed pages, click or tap the Footer drop-down arrow and make a selection.

9. Click or tap the Print button to display the Print dialog box.

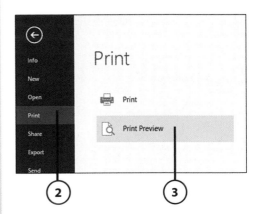

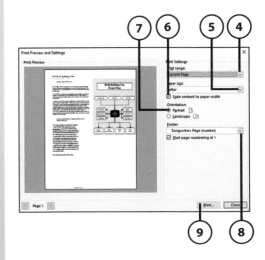

10. Select the printer you want to use; click or tap a printer from the list.

11. To print more than one copy, enter the number of copies you want to print.

12. Click or tap the Print button to print your notes.

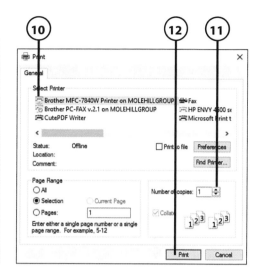

Exporting Notes

OneNote enables you to export your notes into other file formats, including Microsoft Word documents and Adobe PDF files. This way you and others can read (and sometimes edit) your notes in other applications.

You can export a single page, section, or complete notebook to the following file formats:

- Word document (.docx)
- Word 97-2003 document (.doc)
- PDF (.pdf)
- XPS (.xps)
- Single file web page (.mht)
- OneNote 2010-2016 section (.one)
- OneNote Package (.onepkg)

You can export an entire notebook, too, but it can only be exported into PDF, XPS, and OneNote Package formats.

PDF Files

Most computers, tablets, and smartphones today can easily read PDF files, which makes this format ideal for sharing with others on their devices.

Export to a Different File Format

You can export a notebook using the Export options in Backstage view. Pages and sections can be exported into all formats except OneNote Package. Entire notebooks can be exported into only PDF, XPS, and OneNote Package formats.

1. Click or tap the File tab.

2. Click or tap Export to display export options.

3. In the Export Current section, click or tap what you want to export—Page, Section, or Notebook.

4. In the Select Format section, select the file format to which you want to export.

5. Click the Export button to display the Save As dialog box.

6. Select where you want to save the exported file.

7. Click the Save button.

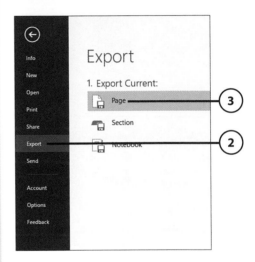

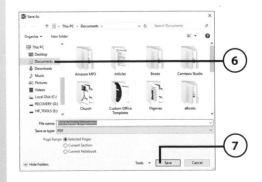

Emailing Notes

Any notes you take can be emailed to anyone with a valid email address. You can send a notes page as an email message, send an entire notebook as a OneNote file attached to an email message, or send an entire notebook as a PDF file attached to a message.

OneNote uses your default email program to send your notes via email. So, for example, if you use Microsoft Outlook for email, the new message is opened in Outlook.

Email a Page

If you need to share only a page of notes with someone, the best option is to email those notes as the body text in a new email message. No attachments are necessary.

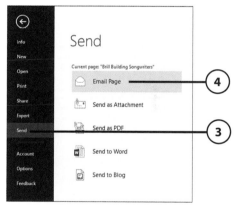

1. Navigate to the page of notes you want to email.

2. Click or tap the File tab.

3. Click or tap Send to display sending options.

4. Click or tap Email Page to open a new email message.

5. The notes from the current page are displayed as the text of the email message. Enter the recipient's email address into the To box.

6. OneNote automatically uses the page title as the message subject; to use a different subject heading, type a new subject heading.

7. Click or tap the Send button to send the message.

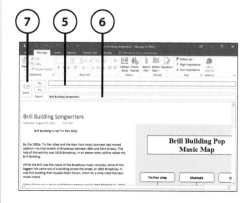

Email a Notebook as an Attachment

If you want to send an entire note-book via email, OneNote lets you do that, too. The notebook file is sent as an attachment to an email message, along with a single-page web file version of the notebook. Recipients can click or tap either attachment to view the notebook in OneNote or as a web page in their web browsers.

1. Click or tap the File tab.

2. Click or tap Send to display sending options.

3. Click or tap Send as Attachment to open a new email message.

4. The email message has two files attached—a OneNote file and a single-page web file (.mht extension). Enter the recipient's email address into the To box.

5. OneNote automatically uses the page title as the message subject; to use a different subject heading, type a new subject heading.

6. Enter any accompanying message text.

7. Click or tap the Send button to send the message.

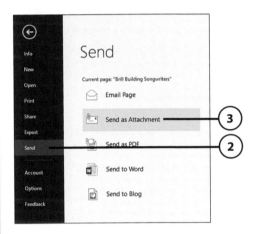

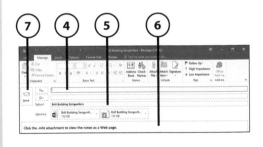

Email a PDF File as an Attachment

While not every person you work with will have the OneNote app installed, most will have the Adobe Acrobat app, which can be used to view PDF files. Sending your notebook as a PDF file might be a safer way to go than sending the file in native OneNote format.

1. Click or tap the File tab.

2. Click or tap Send to display sending options.

3. Click or tap Send as PDF to open a new email message.

4. The email message has a PDF version of your notebook attached. Enter the recipient's email address into the To box.

5. OneNote automatically uses the page title as the message subject; to use a different subject heading, type a new subject heading.

6. Enter any accompanying message text, if needed.

7. Click or tap the Send button to send the message.

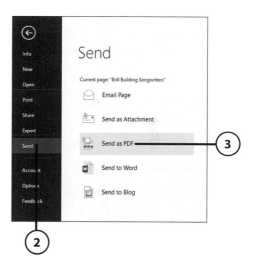

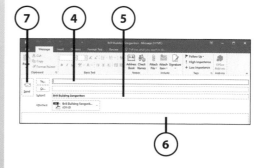

Sharing Notebooks

When you're working on a group project, you might want to share notes with the others in your group. You could take separate notes and share them using any of the emailing or exporting methods described previously in this chapter. Or you could all take notes in the same notebook, thus collaborating together.

To share a notebook, that notebook must be saved to OneDrive, Microsoft's cloud storage service. You can then choose to let others edit a shared notebook, or only view it without being able to make changes (read only).

When you share a notebook for editing, each user has his or her comments displayed in a different color. This way you can keep track of who added what as the project proceeds.

Share via OneDrive

You cannot share a notebook stored locally on your computer. A shared notebook must be stored online, using Microsoft's OneDrive cloud storage service. Learn more about storing your notebooks on OneDrive in Chapter 14, "Taking OneNote Online."

Share a Notebook with Others

If your notebook is stored on Microsoft OneDrive, you can invite others to share your notes. OneNote sends an email invitation to users you specify; the email contains a link to the shared notebook.

You can opt to have users view or edit your notebook. Viewers can look at your notes but not edit them in any way. Users with editing privileges can add their own notes to your notebook, and you see all notes from all users when you access the notebook.

1. Click or tap the File tab.

2. Click or tap Share to display sharing options.

3. Click or tap Share with People to display the Share with People settings.

4. Enter the email address of the people you want to share with. (If a person is in your contacts list, you can simply enter his or her name instead.)

5. Click or tap the Edit/View button and select whether the person Can View (read only) the notebook or Can Edit the notebook.

6. If you want to include a personal message in the invitation, enter that message in the large text box.

7. If you want the user to sign in before accessing the note-book (this helps weeds out unauthorized users), check the Require User to Sign In Before Accessing Document box.

8. Click or tap the Share button. An invitation is sent to the selected user(s).

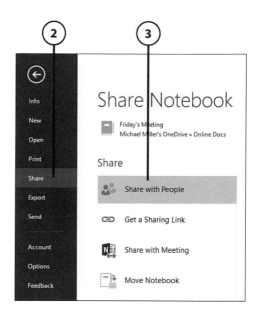

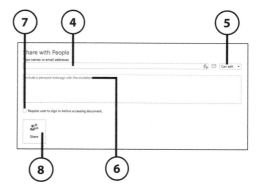

Share a Link to a Notebook

You can also include a link to a shared notebook in an email message, in a social network or blog post, or on your own website. Anyone clicking the link receives access to the notebook. (You can specify either view-only or editing access.)

1. On the Ribbon, click or tap the File tab.

2. Click or tap Share to display sharing options.

3. Click or tap Get a Sharing Link to display the Get a Sharing Link settings.

4. To create a link to let people view (and not edit) the notebook, click or tap the Create Link button under the View Link heading.

5. To create a link to let people edit the notebook, click or tap the Create Link button under the Edit Link heading.

6. Select the link you want to share.

7. Right-click the highlighted link and click or tap Copy, or press Ctrl+C.

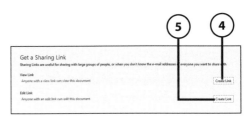

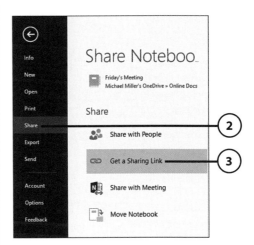

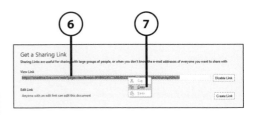

8. Open the email, post, or document where you want to insert the link.

9. Right-click or press and hold and select Paste, or press Ctrl+V.

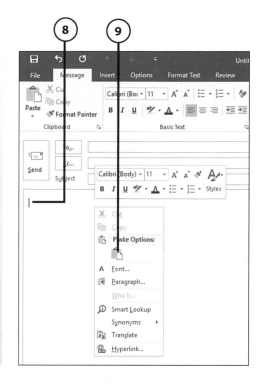

It's Not All Good

Public Sharing

If you post a link to a notebook publicly, anyone with access to that link can see your notes. If you want to keep your notes private, don't share the link publicly.

Access a Shared Notebook

Users who receive an invitation to share a notebook need only click the link in the email to get going. Users can access the notebook via their own copy of OneNote, or via the OneNote Online app in their web browsers.

1. In the invitation email, click or tap View in OneDrive.

2. If prompted to sign in to OneDrive, fill in the appropriate information as needed.

3. You now see the shared notebook in OneNote Online. You can view and/or add new notes as normal.

4. If you are editing in OneNote Online and want to instead view and/or edit this notebook in OneNote 2016, click or tap Open in OneNote.

Free Cloud Storage

If you don't yet have a OneDrive account, it's easy to create one. It's free. OneDrive is Microsoft's online cloud storage service, part of your Microsoft Account. You can use OneDrive to store up to 15GB of data, including OneNote notebooks. To learn more about using OneDrive with OneNote notebooks, see Chapter 14.

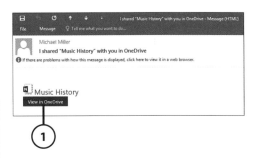

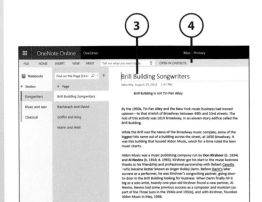

View Changes by Other Users

When more than one user is editing a notebook, each user's changes are identified by their names or initials. You can easily work through the notebook to view the changes made by other users and use the tools on the History tab to help you.

1. By default, you see changes identified by user. (OneNote calls them *authors*.)

2. To hide changes, click or tap the History tab.

3. Click or tap Hide Authors to toggle the display off. To display user identification again, click or tap to toggle the Hide Authors button on.

4. Notes by other authors are identified by that person's initials. Move the mouse pointer over a set of initials to view the other user's full name and when the note was edited.

5. Notes you haven't yet read are shaded in the notebook. To view the next unread note, click or tap the Next Unread button on the History tab.

6. To mark a note as read, move to that note and then click or tap Mark as Read on the History tab, then click or tap Mark as Read. (Alternatively, you can press Ctrl+Q on the keyboard.)

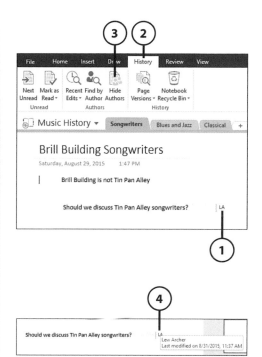

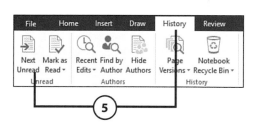

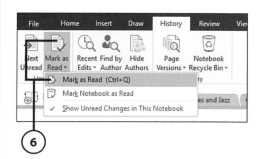

7. To mark a note you've read as unread, move to that note and click or tap Mark as Read on the History tab; then select Mark as Unread.

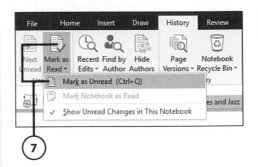

View Most Recent Edits

If a shared notebook is particularly active, you may want to quickly view the most recent edits made.

1. Click or tap the History tab.

2. Click or tap Recent Edits.

3. Select the time period you want to view.

4. OneNote opens the Search Results pane with the most recent edits listed. Click or tap an edit to view it in the notebook.

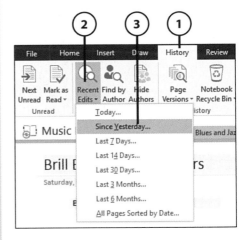

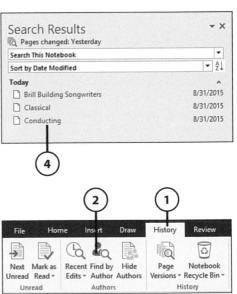

View Edits by User

When multiple users are editing a notebook, it may be useful to view edits made by a specific user.

1. To find all edits from a specific user, click or tap the History tab.

2. Click or tap Find by Author.

3. OneNote opens the Search Results pane with all authors listed. Click or tap an author to display all of this person's edits.

4. Click or tap an edit to go to that note in the notebook.

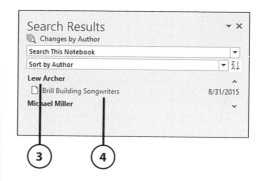

Work with Page Versions

With multiple users contributing to a shared notebook, important notes may sometimes get lost in the flurry of new notes. OneNote lets you quickly return to previous versions of any page, so you can revisit the past state of your notebook and even compare different versions.

1. Click or tap the History tab.

2. Click or tap the Page Versions drop-down arrow to display a list of options.

3. Click or tap Page Versions.

4. The Page pane lists all versions of the page, along with the author of that version. Click or tap a version to view it in the notebook.

5. To delete previous versions, click or tap the Page Versions drop-down arrow on the History tab.

6. Click or tap either Delete All Versions in Section, Delete All Versions in Section Group, or Delete All Versions in Notebook.

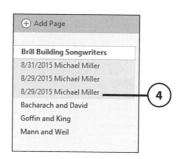

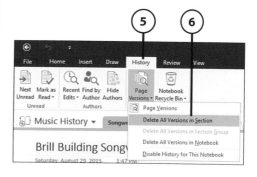

Synchronize Notebooks

When you're sharing a notebook with others, it's possible that more than one person may be editing the notebook at the same time. This is possible because the notebook is stored on the cloud in Microsoft OneDrive. OneNote automatically keeps your notebook in sync at all times; when one person makes a change, it's reflected on the other user's screen within a few seconds.

If you are working offline, however, or if you had an interruption in your Internet service, you may want or need to manually synchronize your notebooks. OneNote lets you do this.

1. Click or tap the File tab.

2. Click or tap Info to display Notebook Information.

3. Click or tap the View Sync Status button.

4. The Shared Notebook Synchronization dialog box opens; click or tap the Sync Now button for the notebook you want to synchronize.

5. Click or tap the Sync All button to synchronize all your notebooks.

6. Click or tap Close to exit the dialog box.

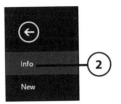

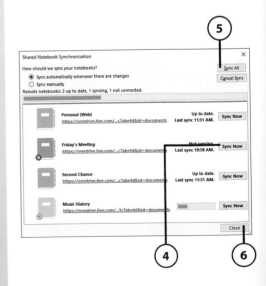

Change Sharing Options

You can add new collaborators to a notebook at any time. You can also remove other users from the notebook, by changing the notebook's sharing options.

1. Click or tap the File tab.

2. Click or tap Share to display sharing options.

3. Click or tap Share with People to display the Share with People settings.

4. Scroll to the Shared With section to view who is currently sharing this notebook and their sharing status (viewing or editing).

5. Right-click or press and hold a user's name and then click or tap Change Permission to change the editing/viewing status.

6. Right-click or press and hold a user's name and then click Remove User to no longer allow sharing with this user.

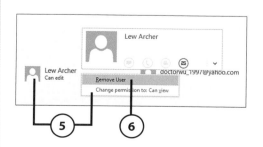

7. The Shared With section also displays viewing and/or editing links for this notebook. Right-click or press and hold a given link and then click or tap Disable Link to no longer allow access to users with this link.

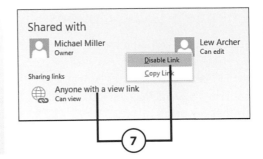

>>>Go Further

SHARE WITH MEETING

If your company uses Outlook or Lync (Skype for Business) to schedule and conduct online meetings, you can use OneNote to take group meeting notes.

Click or tap the File tab and then click Share to display the sharing options. Click or tap Share with Meeting; then click or tap the Share with Meeting button. When the Share Notes with an Online Meeting dialog box appears, click or tap the meeting name and then click or tap OK. You can now take notes that are shared with other users in the same meeting.

Use the OneNote Options dialog box to find
a variety of customization settings.

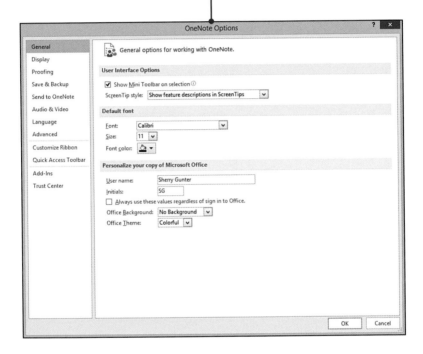

In this chapter, you learn how to apply a few customizing tasks to make OneNote suit the way you like to work. Topics include

→ Finding OneNote's customizing settings
→ Changing the notebook page backgrounds
→ Customizing the Quick Access toolbar
→ Downloading program updates

Customizing OneNote

When you first start using OneNote, all the main features and tools are ready to go right out of the gate. But the more you work with the program, the more you find yourself wanting to tweak a few settings or change a few onscreen elements or add your own personality to OneNote's appearance. You can find a variety of ways to customize OneNote to work the way you want, ranging from changing the default note font to adding your own toolbar buttons. In this chapter, you learn a few customizing techniques to get you started.

Finding Customizing Options

If you're looking for the behind-the-scenes customizing settings, the OneNote Options dialog box is the place to go. The OneNote Options dialog box is chock-full of settings, from display settings to language settings, from proofing settings to advanced settings. Options and settings are listed in 12 different categories, each with its own unique check boxes, radio buttons, drop-down menus, and text boxes to fill in and select. Many of OneNote's features are turned on by default, while others are not. You can visit the dialog box to enable or disable features.

In this chapter, you learn about changing a few of OneNote's settings, such as the default font and size used for text notes. It's a good idea to scan through all the various options available in the Options dialog box. You may encounter other settings that can greatly enhance your OneNote experience.

Customize the Default Note Font

A basic setting you might want to change right away in OneNote is the default font and size used for note text. OneNote assigns 11-point Calibri as the font for every new note you insert. You can change the setting to make the note text more legible or suit the way you want your notebooks to appear.

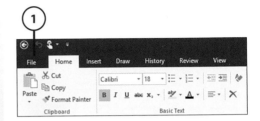

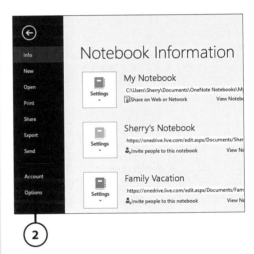

1. Click or tap File.

2. Click or tap Options.

3. Click or tap General if it isn't already selected.

4. Under the Default font heading, click or tap the Font drop-down arrow.

5. Click or tap another font to use.

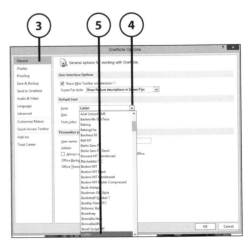

Font Tips

Legibility is a big issue, especially if you have trouble reading your notes on the computer or device you normally work with. If you need to fit more notes onto a screen, such as a smartphone, you may need to try a slightly smaller font size. If you work primarily on a computer or laptop, a larger font size makes a big difference. If you don't like the new setting, you can also change it back or try another.

6. Click or tap the Size drop-down arrow.

7. Click or tap the size you want to use.

8. Click or tap OK to exit the dialog box and apply the changes.

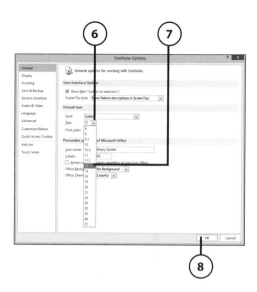

Customize Backups

OneNote is set up to automatically back up your notebooks regularly every week. Depending on your work, you may want to back up notebooks at a different interval, such as every other day or every two weeks. You can make changes to the backup frequency through the Save & Backup category in the Options dialog box.

1. Click or tap File.

2. Click or tap Options.

Change Folder Locations

Also found in the Save & Backup category are options for changing where default OneNote folders are saved. You can click or tap the Modify button if you want to change a selected folder's location. Always use caution when changing folder locations; it may cause confusion later when trying to find where things are relocated.

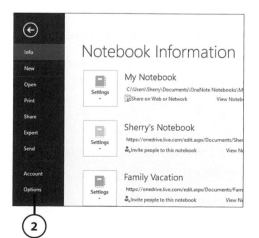

3. Click or tap Save & Backup.

4. Under the Backup heading, click or tap the Automatically Back Up My Notebook at the Following Time Interval drop-down arrow.

5. Click or tap another interval time to use.

6. Click or tap OK to exit the dialog box and apply the changes.

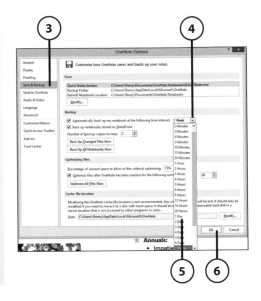

Changing the Page Setup

You can customize the way you view certain page elements in your notebooks using the features found on the Ribbon's View tab. For example, you can hide the default page titles to free up more onscreen room for working with notes. Or how about turning on rule lines so your notebooks look more like real notebook paper, or making your pages look like grid paper? All the Page Setup commands located on the View tab can be turned on or off as you work to suit your own style.

Hide the Page Title

Hiding the page title can really free up some onscreen real estate. The downside is the page tab then grabs text from the first note on the page to name the tab. If you're not too picky about page tab names, hiding the title can be a good idea.

1. Click or tap View.

2. Click or tap Hide Page Title.

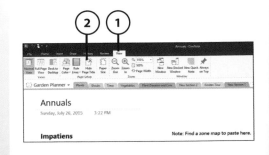

3. A warning prompt appears letting you know the page title, date, and time stamp will be deleted; click or tap Yes to continue.

4. OneNote hides the page title at the top of the page.

5. The first note's text is used as the page tab name.

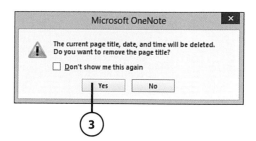

3

One Page at a Time

The Hide Page Title command works only for the current page. It does not affect other page titles. You have to activate the Hide Page Title command again to make the next page's title disappear.

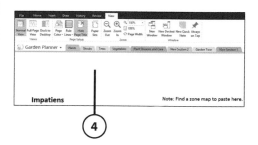

4

Restoring the Time and Date

If you hide the page title and click or tap the Hide Page Title button again, the date and time stamp appear and the title area remains blank. You can type in a new title, if needed.

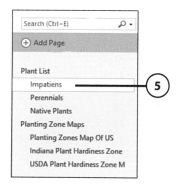

5

Display Rule Lines

A great way to change page appearance is to display rule lines or grids. Not only does a linear background look nice, it's also a great way to help you keep your notes lined up and orderly.

1. Click or tap View.

2. Click or tap the Rule Lines drop-down arrow.

3. Click or tap a page line style from the menu.

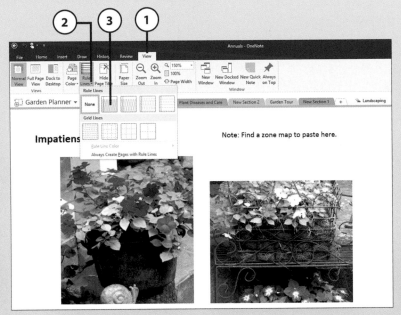

>>>Go Further

MAKE IT THE DEFAULT

If you find a rule or grid line style you like a lot, you can make it the default page background. With the style already applied to the current page, click or tap the Rule Lines drop-down arrow and choose Always Create Pages with Rule Lines. Any new pages you add also feature the rule or grid line style.

4. OneNote applies the line style you selected; you can move notes to line up with the rule lines, if desired.

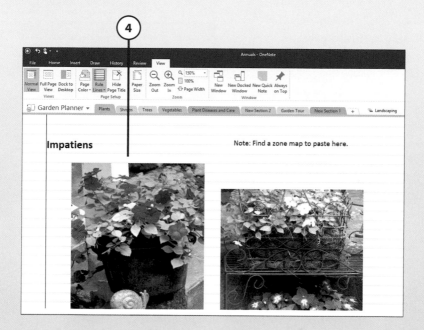

Return to the Default Style

If you want to reset a page to the default blank style again, click or tap the Rule Lines drop-down arrow and choose None from the menu.

Change the Paper Size

Yet another customizing option you might try out is changing the paper size. By default, OneNote sets your note pages with a Portrait layout (shorter width, longer length) and inner margins at 0.5 at the top and bottom of the page, and 1.0 at the right and left sides. You can change these settings to suit the way you work or how you like to print out notes. You can also customize these settings and reuse them as a page template.

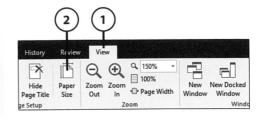

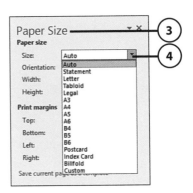

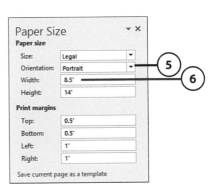

1. Click or tap View.

2. Click or tap Paper Size.

3. OneNote opens the Paper Size pane; you can use this pane to set page options for display and for printing.

4. Click or tap the Size drop-down arrow and choose a paper size.

5. If applicable, click or tap the Orientation drop-down arrow and choose an orientation.

6. If setting a custom page, fill out the page width and height boxes.

7. To adjust page margins, edit the margin settings. OneNote adjusts the page with each new setting you change.

8. Click or tap Close to close the Paper Size pane.

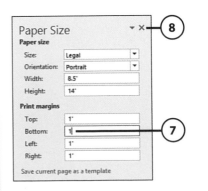

Save It as a Template

To save your new paper size settings as a page template, click or tap the Save Current Page as a Template link in the Paper Size pane and give the template a unique name.

Customizing the Quick Access Toolbar

You can customize toolbars in OneNote to suit the way you work and the type of commands you commonly use. Although the programmers and developers of OneNote tried to anticipate all kinds of usage, there are always exceptions to the common settings. For example, if you want a Delete button more readily available, you can add one to the Quick Access toolbar so it's always ready to use. The same is true for any particular command or feature you need to place front-and-center.

Although you can customize the Ribbon and its many tabs, you may prefer to customize the Quick Access toolbar with your favorite features since it always sits at the top of the program window. You may find it easier to access commands on this particular toolbar, unlike the Ribbon where commands and features are organized on tabs that you have to click to view and utilize. The steps for customizing the Ribbon are similar to those for customizing the Quick Access toolbar, however, just in case you want to pursue some additional customizing options later.

Add Your Favorite Command

Customizing the Quick Access toolbar is easier than you think. The only difficult part is deciding what command or feature you want to place on the toolbar.

1. Click or tap the Customize Quick Access Toolbar button.

2. Click or tap More Commands.

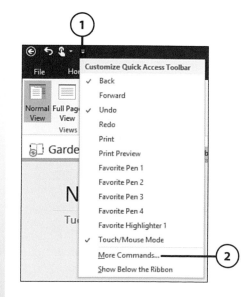

3. OneNote opens the OneNote Options dialog box to the Quick Access Toolbar settings.

4. Click or tap the command you want to add.

5. Click or tap the Add button.

6. The command is listed on the toolbar.

7. To change the order of the commands, select a command and click or tap the Move Up or Move Down arrow to move the command's position in the toolbar.

8. Click or tap OK to exit the dialog box and apply the change.

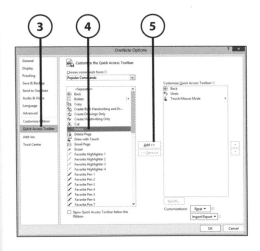

Turning On Commands

The Quick Access toolbar already features a few popular commands, but they aren't shown on the toolbar. You can activate them with a click. Just click or tap the Customize Quick Access Toolbar button and select which button you want to add to the display.

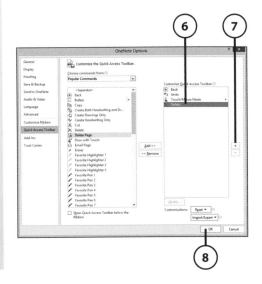

It's Not All Good

Where's My Command?

If you're having trouble locating the command or feature you want to add, try clicking or tapping the Choose Commands From drop-down arrow in the Options dialog box and pick a command category. The left column then lists commands normally associated with the chosen category.

Updating the OneNote Program

Do you like to keep your Microsoft Office programs up to date? You can control how often updates occur in OneNote, or perform a manual update to make sure all the latest program fixes and tweaks are applied. Any time you want to execute a manual update, visit OneNote's Account page. Here you find user information, licensing or subscription information, and update options, as well as settings for changing the Office theme or background.

Update OneNote

You can carry out a manual update to download and install the latest fixes and program tweaks. By default, the Microsoft Office programs are set up to perform automatic updates, but you can run a manual update when you want to check for program changes and upgrades.

1. Click or tap File.

2. Click or tap Account.

3. Click or tap Update Options.

4. Click or tap Update Now.

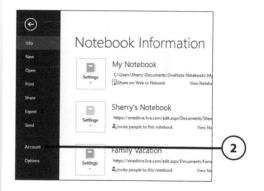

5. OneNote checks for updates and downloads and installs any updates it finds. Depending on the update, you might be prompted to exit OneNote and restart the program or computer to complete any update installation.

6. When the updates are complete, click or tap Close.

Disable Updates

If you prefer not to run automatic updates, you can click or tap the Disable Updates option in the Update Options drop-down list.

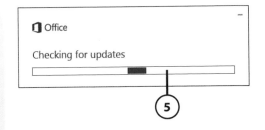

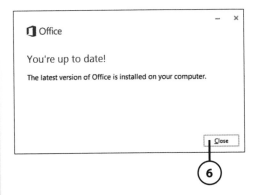

Use OneDrive to store your notebooks to the cloud.

Folder

OneNote notebook

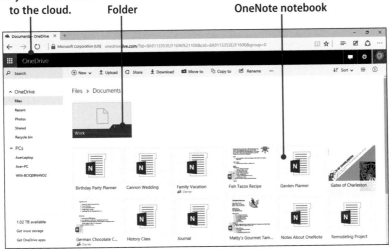

In this chapter, you learn how to use OneNote's online features and make use of Microsoft's cloud storage and cloud computing options. Topics include

→ Discovering how OneDrive works
→ Moving a computer notebook to your cloud storage account
→ Using the OneDrive desktop app
→ Exploring how Microsoft's OneNote Online web-based app works

Taking OneNote Online

OneNote isn't just a static app that stays in one spot. You can take it—and all the notebooks you use—on the road, whether that means traveling far and wide, or out and about around your home, office, or school. As long as you have an Internet connection, you can continue working on notebooks. An essential part of OneNote's online features is Microsoft's OneDrive file hosting site. Free with your Microsoft account, you can use OneDrive as a virtual hard drive, storing your notebooks in the cloud and making them accessible across devices. You can also use OneNote Online, Microsoft's web-based version of OneNote. In this chapter, you learn how to make use of cloud computing to store your notebooks online, and make use of the Microsoft OneNote Online web app.

Using OneDrive with OneNote

OneDrive is Microsoft's online cloud storage service. Formerly known as SkyDrive, OneDrive is free with a Microsoft account and lets you store up to 15GB of data. You can add additional storage for a fee, such as 100GB for $1.99 a month or 200GB for $3.99 a month.

As a file hosting site, OneDrive allows users to store all kinds of files, including OneNote notebooks, and access them from any web browser, computer, or mobile device. You can easily sync your files across platforms and devices, share them with other people, and manage the files any way you want. OneDrive is also a great way to back up your notebook files. It acts rather like a virtual hard drive.

If you aren't already using OneDrive, it's easy to get started. As part of your Microsoft account, your OneDrive storage is ready and waiting. There are two ways to use OneDrive: OneDrive's web-based app or the OneDrive app on your computer or device. You can navigate to the OneDrive website (OneDrive.live.com) to view online content using your browser window. You may be prompted to sign in to your Microsoft account first.

The OneDrive web app uses a folder system interface much like your own computer's hard drive. You can view various files in your folders, add and rename folders and files, upload files, sync files between computers and devices, and share files and folders with others. OneDrive starts you out with several default folders, such as Documents and Pictures. You can add more folders as needed, rename them, and move files around between folders.

Main folders are listed here.   **Folders**

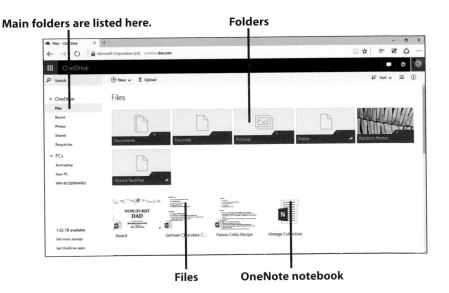

Files   **OneNote notebook**

A folder "tree" pane lists main folders on the left side of the app window, and an area for viewing folders and contents sits on the right. As you're browsing your files on the OneDrive site, folders appear bright blue and files appear as thumbnail images of their content. You can use the tools and commands at the top of the window to add new folders, upload files, sort files, and more. By default, Microsoft OneNote stores your notebook files in the top level Files folder on OneDrive.

If you open a notebook stored in the cloud while in OneDrive, the OneNote Online web-based app opens and displays your notebook file. You can use the online app and its tools to work with the notebook. If you prefer using the full-featured OneNote program on your computer, you can switch over to your desktop version of the program.

Your notebooks are automatically synced for you whenever there are changes to the contents. For example, if you're working on a notebook on your laptop, any changes you make are automatically reflected in the notebook's location on OneDrive. If you don't have an Internet connection at the time, OneNote keeps track of the changes and updates them the next time you have an Internet connection.

OneNote Online web app

>>>*Go Further*

WHAT IS THE CLOUD?

The cloud is a secure, private storage area on the Internet, but more specifically, it's the ability to store and process computer data online rather than on your own computer. Cloud connectivity is really twofold—one part is *cloud storage*, taking your files and saving them to dedicated web servers. The other part is *cloud computing*, which is being able to run a computer program hosted on a web server. Both parts offer many advantages, and both are available through your Microsoft account.

Large companies, such as Microsoft, have server "farms" or data centers, filled with thousands of servers. They work by offering you space on their servers to store all types of files. (Web servers are computers that host websites, storage, and applications.) Your Microsoft account includes cloud storage through OneDrive.

Cloud computing uses the Web as a platform for applications. Microsoft Office Online and Office 365 are examples of cloud computing. Users can create word processing documents, slide show presentations, spreadsheets, notebooks, and more, using web programs. OneNote Online is a web-based app.

You can also use the OneDrive app found on your computer or device to access cloud storage items and web-based Microsoft Office apps. The app presents the OneDrive folder system on your computer or device. Here's how to find the OneDrive app depending on your operating system or device:

Windows 10   You can find the OneDrive app on the Start menu's All apps list.

Windows 8 and 8.1   OneDrive appears as a tile on the Start screen.

Windows 7   If you have the OneDrive desktop app installed, it's listed as Microsoft OneDrive on the Start menu; click or tap All Programs to find it.

Mac   Locate the program icon on the Dock.

Tablet or smartphone   Look for the OneDrive app listed among all your installed apps.

OneDrive desktop app   Online folders and files are listed here.

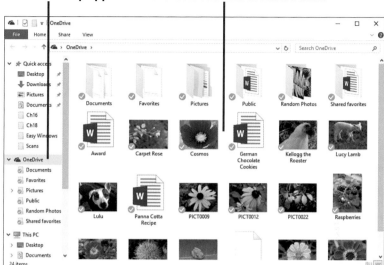

When you open the OneDrive app, it shows your synced folders and files in the File Explorer window. Remember, the files aren't actually on your own computer, but rather, they're cached (temporary content storage) copies of what's on your cloud storage. If you open a notebook through the OneDrive desktop app, your web browser opens the notebook in the OneNote Online web-based app. If you prefer to open a notebook using the OneNote program on your computer, you can open the program window first and then open the notebook you want to use. You can also right-click or press and hold the OneNote filename on OneDrive and choose Open in OneNote.

>>>*Go Further*

ONEDRIVE FOR OLDER OPERATING SYSTEMS

Windows cloud service has been around since 2007 and the name has changed a couple of times—Windows Live Folders, Windows Live SkyDrive, then shortened to SkyDrive, and now OneDrive. All you need to use the service is a free Microsoft account. If you're using Windows 10 or 8.1, OneDrive is already integrated with the operating system. OneDrive comes preinstalled with both operating systems. For example, when you open the File Explorer window to view your files and folders, OneDrive is listed as one of the storage options available.

If you're a Windows 7 user, you don't have to miss out on this fabulous feature just because you're using an older OS version. You can download and install the OneDrive desktop application on your computer and OneDrive shows up in your listing of storage locations. Using your web browser, visit the onedrive.live.com web page to download and install the app or find it available in the Windows Store. The download page also offers options for downloading the app to Android, Mac, iPad, Windows Phone, and Xbox devices.

Note: The OneDrive desktop app is not available for Windows XP or Linux.

Sign In to OneDrive with Your Browser

You can sign in to the OneDrive website to view notebooks—and other files—you have stored in the cloud. OneDrive lists your stored files in a folder hierarchy much like File Explorer (Windows) or Finder (Mac).

1. With your favorite browser window open, type in the URL onedrive.live.com and press Enter/Return.

2. The OneDrive start page may appear; type in your Microsoft account ID if required.

3. Type in your password.

4. Click or tap Sign In.

5. OneDrive lists any files and folders you have stored on your cloud storage account; Files is the top level folder displayed.

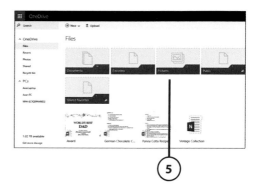

Stay Signed In

You can keep yourself signed in by clicking or tapping the Keep Me Signed In check box on the OneDrive start page. Doing so lets you skip the sign in process the next time you open the website. This option is recommended only if you're using a private computer or device.

View OneDrive Folders and Files

You can open folders in OneDrive and view their contents at a glance. Files you see listed are thumbnail images representative of their actual content or files may be represented by their application icon. OneNote files are listed with the OneNote icon.

1. To open a folder from the OneDrive page, click or tap the folder icon.

2. Notice that the folder contents appear as thumbnail images.

3. Identify the notebooks by the OneNote icon.

4. You can use the toolbar commands to work with online files and folders.

5. To apply commands to a specific folder or file, click or tap the corner of the file icon or thumbnail to apply a selection check mark.

6. Click or tap the View button to switch between viewing files as tiles (the default view) or as a list.

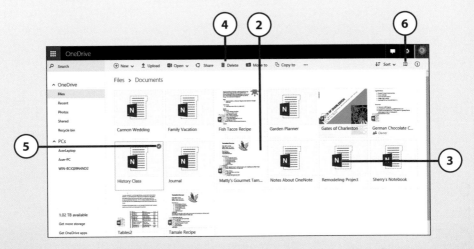

7. Details view displays folder contents as a list of filenames.

8. Navigate to any of the main OneDrive folders using the folder pane.

9. Use the browser window's navigation buttons to move back and forth between open folders.

10. Click or tap OneDrive to return to the top level folder.

11. Click or tap a file to open it in its corresponding web app.

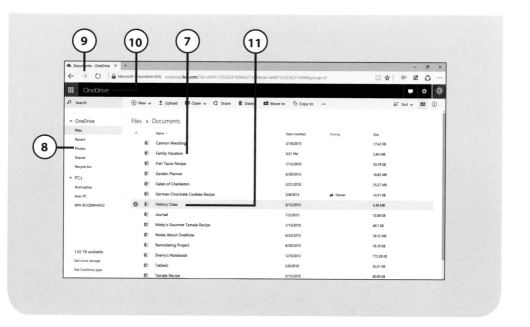

Open a OneDrive Notebook in OneNote 2016

You can easily open a OneNote notebook you are currently storing on OneDrive and work with it in the OneNote 2016 program window on your computer.

1. From the OneDrive web app, navigate to the notebook you want to use.

2. Right-click or press and hold the notebook name to reveal a pop-up menu.

3. Click or tap Open in OneNote.

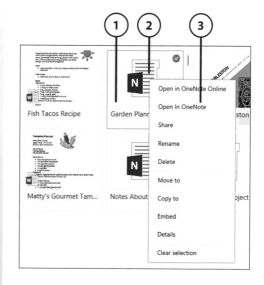

4. The OneNote program installed on your computer opens the notebook file.

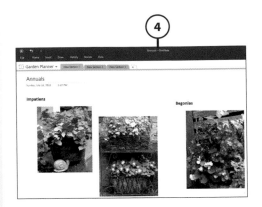

Relocate an Online Notebook from OneDrive to Your Computer

You can move a notebook stored in the cloud and relocate it onto your computer. This technique helps you keep the content but remove it from OneDrive. Unfortunately, you must move a notebook section-by-section to do so.

1. From the OneNote program window, click or tap the File tab on the Ribbon.

2. Click or tap New.

3. Click or tap This PC.

4. Assign a name for the new notebook.

5. Click or tap Create Notebook.

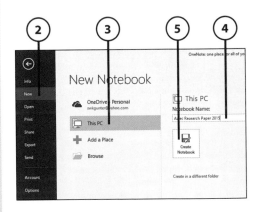

6. Click or tap the Notebooks list.

7. Click or tap the pushpin icon to pin the list in place.

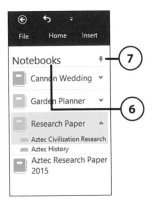

8. Click or tap the notebook you want to move content from.

9. Drag each section of the notebook you want to move and drop it in the new notebook you just created.

10. To remove the notebook from OneDrive, open the OneDrive web app and check the notebook you want to delete (click or tap the upper-right corner of the file's icon to add a check mark).

11. Click or tap Delete and OneDrive permanently removes the notebook file.

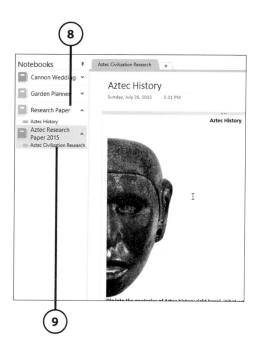

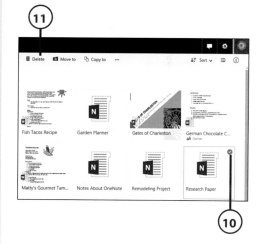

Can I Just Delete It?

You can delete a notebook from OneDrive without keeping the content. Check the notebook file you want to remove and click or tap the Delete icon on the toolbar. The notebook and all its contents are immediately deleted from the web app.

Relocating with the Notebook Properties Dialog Box

You an also relocate a notebook using the Notebook Properties dialog box. Start by opening the notebook in OneNote 2016. Click or tap the Notebooks list, right-click or press and hold the notebook name, and click or tap Properties. In the Notebook Properties dialog box, click or tap Change Location. Navigate to a local folder, and click Select. Lastly, return to OneDrive and delete the notebook listed there.

Manually Sync a Notebook

As you work with cloud-based note-books and make changes online or offline, OneNote syncs them auto-matically the next time you establish an Internet connection. You can also sync your notebooks manually.

1. From the OneNote program window, click or tap the Notebooks list.

2. Right-click or press and hold the notebook name you want to sync to reveal a pop-up menu.

3. Click or tap Sync This Notebook Now.

Configure Manually Syncing

If you prefer to turn off auto-matic syncing, you can configure OneNote to sync manually every time. Right-click or press and hold the notebook name listed in the upper-left corner of the program window. Click or tap Notebook Sync Status. Click or tap the Sync manually option, and then click or tap Close to save the new setting.

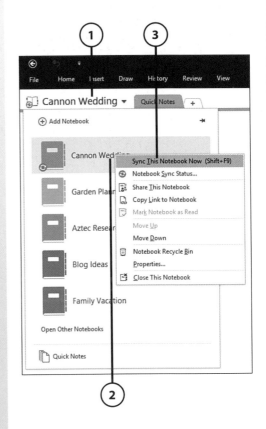

Share a OneDrive Notebook

You can share a OneDrive notebook with other users by inviting them to use the notebook via a link you email to them.

1. From the OneDrive web app, check the notebook file you want to share (click or tap the upper-right corner of the file's icon).

2. Click or tap Share.

3. The Share form opens; type in the email address for the person you want to share with.

4. Optionally, type in a note to add with the invitation.

5. Click or tap Share and the invitation is sent.

6. Click Close.

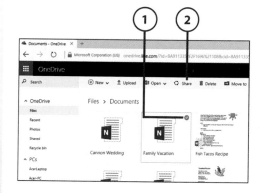

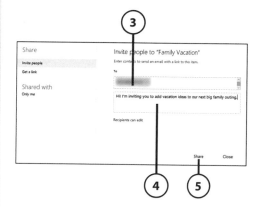

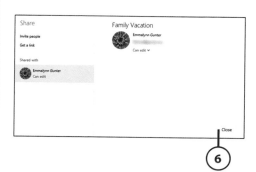

>>>Go Further
TURN OFF SHARING

To turn off a OneDrive notebook's shared status, right-click or press and hold the notebook file icon and click or tap Details from the pop-up menu or if the Info button is in view on the browser window's toolbar, click or tap Info. Either method opens the Info pane. Click or tap the Can Edit link for the person you want to edit to reopen the Share box. Next, click or tap the Can Edit drop-down menu and choose Stop Sharing.

Create a New OneDrive Folder

You can add folders to OneDrive to help keep your files organized. For example, you might place all your work-related notebooks in a Work folder.

1. From the OneDrive web app, click or tap New.

2. Click or tap Folder.

3. Type in a folder name.

4. Click or tap Create.

5. The new file is added to the current folder you were viewing when you activated the command.

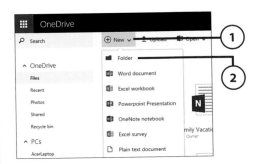

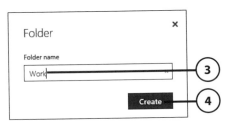

>>>Go Further
RENAME FOLDERS

If you ever want to rename a folder in OneDrive, check the folder (click or tap the upper-right corner of the file's icon) and activate the Rename command. The command is located on the OneDrive toolbar. If it's not in view in your browser window (not all toolbar buttons are displayed if you're using a smaller windows size), you can click or tap the ellipses icon (three dots), and then click or tap Rename. You can also right-click or press and hold the folder icon and choose Rename. Either method opens the Rename box and you can type in a new name and click Rename to make it official.

Move Files Between Folders

You can move files between folders on OneDrive using the Move To command.

1. From the OneDrive web app, check the notebook you want to move.

2. Click or tap Move To.

3. Click or tap the folder you want to move the notebook to.

4. Click or tap Move.

Or Copy It

You can also copy files and paste them into different folders. Click or tap the Copy To button on OneDrive's toolbar to copy a checked file and place it in a different folder.

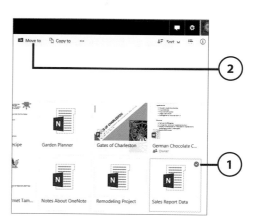

Sign Out of OneDrive

When you finish using the OneDrive web app, you can sign out.

1. Click or tap the Account menu (profile pic).

2. Click or tap Sign Out.

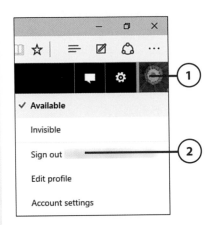

More Account Options

The Account menu also includes commands for editing your Microsoft account profile and general account settings. For example, you can change your Microsoft account picture.

Using the OneDrive Desktop App

Another way to view and access your cloud storage files is using the OneDrive desktop app. The app is built-in for Windows 10 and 8.1 users, and Windows 8 and 7 users can download and install the app from the Windows Store. If you're using another device, such as a tablet or smartphone, you can also download and use the OneDrive app.

Open the OneDrive Desktop App

You can open the OneDrive desktop app to view your online contents. Depending on your device or operating system, the app may appear on your Start menu or among your device's apps. This example shows how to find the app using the Windows 10 Start menu's All Apps list.

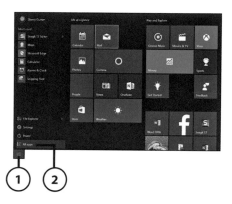

1. Click or tap Start.

2. Click or tap All Apps.

3. Scroll down the list to the OneDrive app.

4. Click or tap OneDrive.

5. The File Explorer window opens to the OneDrive folder display.

Finding the App

If you're using Windows 8.1 or Windows 8, you can look for the OneDrive app as a tile on the Start menu. If you're using Windows 7, OneDrive is listed under All Programs on the Start menu. Mac users can find the app on the Dock. If you're using a tablet or smartphone, you can find OneDrive listed among all your app icons.

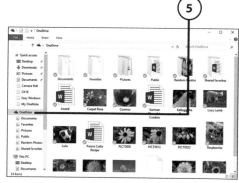

View Folders and Files in the OneDrive Desktop App

The integrated OneDrive desktop app lets you view and work with files and folders stored on your cloud account. The File Explorer window displays OneDrive contents. Any notebook files you open in the OneDrive app open in OneNote Online, so if you open a notebook, OneNote Online opens in your default web browser window to display the file. This task shows the OneDrive app in the Windows 8.1 OS.

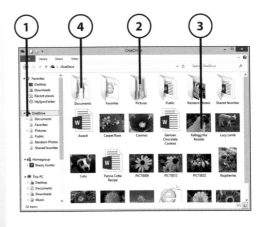

1. You can view the main OneDrive folders in the Folder list pane.

2. You can identify folder icons by their folder-like appearance.

3. You can identify files as thumbnail images.

4. To open a folder, double-click or double-tap the folder name.

5. Click or tap a file to open it in its corresponding web app.

6. To change how files and folders are listed, click or tap the Ribbon's View tab and choose a listing layout from the gallery.

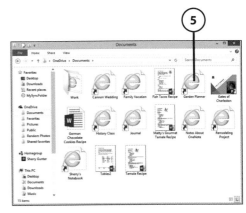

Default Storage

By default, OneNote automatically places any notebooks you save to the cloud in OneDrive's top level folder, labeled Files. You can move notebooks to other folders as needed.

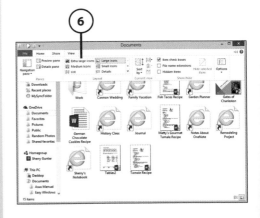

Open a OneDrive Notebook from the OneDrive Desktop App

You can use the OneDrive desktop app to open a cloud-based notebook and work with it in the OneNote Online app.

1. With the OneDrive desktop app open, navigate to the notebook you want to use.

2. Double-click or double-tap the notebook.

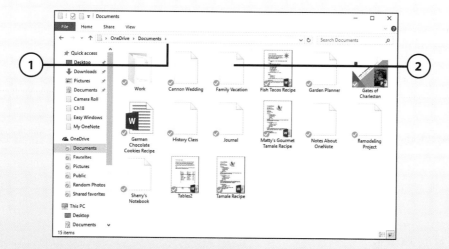

3. The default browser window opens and displays your notebook in the OneNote Online web app.

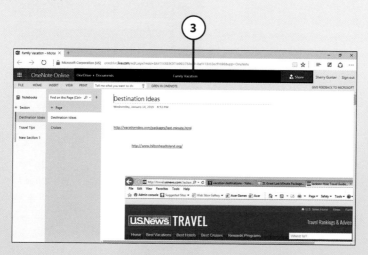

Using the OneNote Online Web App

The OneNote Online web app works much like the desktop version of the program, but without the advanced editing features. For example, OneNote Online does not support older notebook file formats, such as OneNote 2003 or OneNote 2007. Some features, like printing, work a bit differently, too. You can't print a notebook from OneNote Online, but you can use your browser window's Print command instead. All the Microsoft Office web apps are designed for light editing only. For full-blown program features, you need to switch to the desktop applications.

As you learned in the previous tasks in this chapter, you can open OneNote Online automatically when you select a cloud notebook, either from OneDrive's web app or the OneDrive desktop app. You can also open OneNote Online directly and then choose which notebook to use.

Sign In to the OneNote Online App

Another way to open OneNote Online is directly through your web browser. You may be prompted to sign in first using your Microsoft account.

1. Type the URL **www.onenote. com/notebooks** in your web browser window and press Enter/ Return.

2. The OneNote sign in page may appear (if not, skip to step 7).

3. Click or tap Sign In with a Microsoft Account.

4. Type in your Microsoft account ID.

5. Type in your password.

6. Click or tap Sign In.

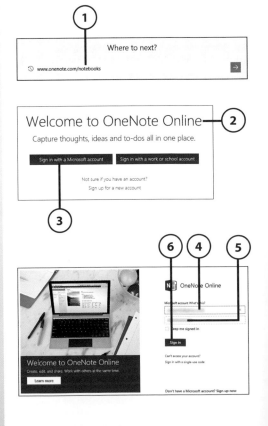

7. The Notebooks page opens; click or tap the notebook you want to view.

8. OneNote Online opens your notebook.

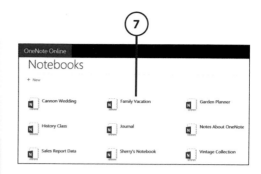

Office Online

The online web apps of the Microsoft Office programs, including OneNote, are free to use. You don't need a subscription. The only caveat is these aren't full-featured versions of the computer software. However, you can buy the complete programs as a subscription plan with Office 365 (with packages for Home, Personal, and Student use) or purchase the software outright.

View the OneNote Online Window

OneNote Online looks similar to the desktop program, but features are displayed a bit differently.

1. To view a section click or tap its name.

2. Click or tap a page name to view its contents.

3. Click the Ribbon tabs to access commands and features.

4. Click or tap Notebooks to return to your available notebooks list.

5. Click or tap OneDrive to view your OneDrive folders and files.

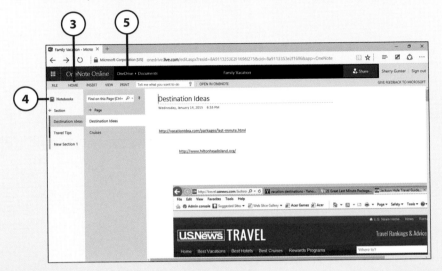

6. Click or tap the List of Microsoft Services button to view a menu of other Office web apps you can use.

7. To add a note, click or tap where you want it inserted and start typing.

8. You can use your browser window's controls to navigate through sections and pages you view, as well refresh a page.

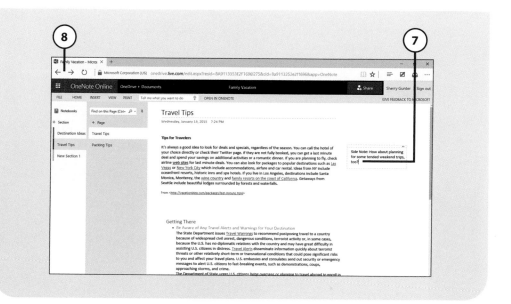

Open a Notebook in the Desktop Program Window

OneNote Online offers several ways you can switch over to the desktop application and work on the notebook using the full functionality of the program. The steps in this task demonstrate using Windows 10's Microsoft Edge browser to open a notebook.

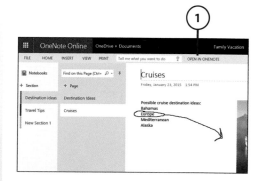

1. Click or tap the Open In OneNote button on the Ribbon.

2. Click or tap Yes in the prompt box.

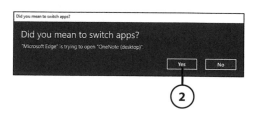

3. The OneNote program window opens and displays the notebook; you can start adding notes or viewing various pages and sections.

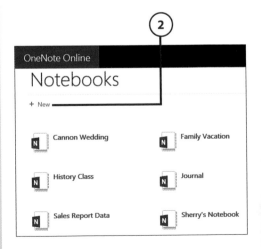

Use the File Menu

Another way to access your desktop program is through the File menu. Click or tap the Ribbon's File menu and then click or tap Open in OneNote.

Open a New Notebook

You can start new notebooks in OneNote Online. New notebooks you create are automatically saved in your cloud storage account.

1. Click or tap Notebooks.

2. Click or tap New.

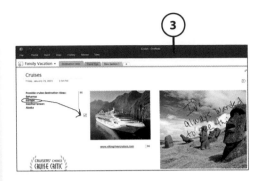

3. Type in a name for the new notebook.

4. Click or tap Create.

5. OneNote Online opens the new notebook.

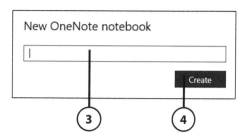

Managing Notebooks

OneNote Online also has short-cuts to OneDrive so you can quickly manage online note-books. From the Notebooks page, click or tap Manage and Delete in the upper-right corner. This opens the OneDrive web app and lists your cloud storage folders and files.

Index

O

More Best-Selling **My** Books!

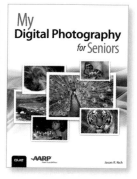

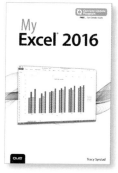

Learning to use your smartphone, tablet, camera, game, or software has never been easier with the full-color My Series. You'll find simple, step-by-step instructions from our team of experienced authors. The organized, task-based format allows you to quickly and easily find exactly what you want to achieve.

Visit quepublishing.com/mybooks to learn more.